YOUR GRIEF, YOUR WAY

A Year of Practical Guidance
and Comfort after Loss

YOUR GRIEF, YOUR WAY

SHELBY FORSYTHIA

ZEITGEIST · NEW YORK

This book is designed to provide helpful information on the subjects discussed. It is not meant to be used for, nor should it take the place of, diagnosing or treating any medical conditions. Please consult a physician or mental health professional before adopting any exercises or guidelines. The publisher and author are not responsible for any specific health needs that may require supervision or consultation with a licensed and qualified healthcare provider.

Published in the United States by Zeitgeist,
an imprint of Zeitgeist™, a division of
Penguin Random House LLC, New York.

penguinrandomhouse.com

Zeitgeist™ is a trademark of Penguin Random House LLC

ISBN: 9780593196717
Ebook ISBN: 9780593196724

Art © Asya_mix/Getty

Book design by Aimee Fleck

Printed in the United States of America

4th Printing

For you,
as you find your way

INTRODUCTION

Welcome to the club nobody wants to join: the Grief Club. I'm so sorry you have a reason to be here. And simultaneously, I'm glad you've picked up this book.

When my mom died suddenly in 2013, I struggled to read. That is to say, I couldn't keep my focus for more than 30 seconds at a time. If a self-help book couldn't give it to me straight in a couple of sentences, its advice was useless to me. I desperately wanted a book that was short, sweet, and powerful—like a rescue inhaler for my grief. Unable to find such a book, I decided to write one.

This book is a simple, fluff-free guide to navigating life after the death of a loved one. While it is designed as a daily guide, with dated entries, know that there is no right or wrong way to read it. You are welcome to jump around, to skip pages, to flip the book open on days when your grief is especially loud or overwhelming. The book features alternating messages of comfort: each page contains a quote about grief and a short paragraph about the quote, along with a practical tip to help you to tend to and process your grief. You'll also find a range of doable exercises in this book, including short meditations, mindful reframings, journaling prompts, and concrete actions. There is absolutely no pressure to agree with the quotes featured in it or to perform the practical tasks. As with any message you receive in life after loss, take what works for you and discard the rest. Not everything will apply to your grief right now, and that's okay.

You may want to work through the exercises with a trusted friend, or keep this book tucked away in your nightstand or glove compartment. It's normal to want to "do grief" out in the open, and it's also normal to keep your healing process lovingly protected behind closed doors. There is no right or wrong way to heal.

It is my hope that this book will act as a lighthouse for you in the darkness of loss. Whether you're fresh into life after the death of a loved one or you're feeling isolated and alone because the rest of the world has moved on, know that you are seen and heard in your pain. In my four years of working one-on-one with grieving clients, interviewing grief experts and authors on my podcast *Coming Back*, and writing about grief and loss, I've witnessed the extraordinary heartache of others and have had the honor of sharing a bit of my own. I've walked in shoes similar to yours, and I designed this book as a friend and companion to you in the midst of heartache. There is no one-size-fits-all solution to grief; there is only the recognition that everyone grieves. You are absolutely not alone.

This book does not ask you to follow any set structure. (It is your grief, your way, after all!) As you read it, my only ask is that you pay attention to your grief. Doing so will help you stay openhearted through life's most heartbreaking experience: loss.

With love and so much more,
Shelby Forsythia

"Be willing to be a beginner every single morning." – MEISTER ECKHART

Each new day, each new year, is an opportunity to be a student of life. It's humbling to assume the role of beginner, especially as you age, but doing so can help you see your life, your friends and family, and your grief through fresh eyes. Admitting the very human truth that you don't know everything allows you to remain curious and engaged instead of closed off. Being willing to be a beginner is not about being naïve or unwise; it's about being open to learning something new every single day.

JANUARY 2

MANY recovery programs advise taking life "one day at a time." This phrase is helpful when you're reeling in the overwhelming anxiety of figuring out how to "do grief" in the long term. Consider coming up with a mantra that encourages you to take life after loss one day at a time. Some of my favorites are "Just do the next right thing," "I have everything I need in this moment," and as my quirky middle school science teacher used to say, "All will be revealed." These supportive one-sentence mantras are grounding reminders that your goal in grief is not to figure out the Entire Rest of Your Life in one sitting, but to make it through today. For an extra boost, write your mantra down and hang it where you'll see it often—over a desk, on a bathroom mirror, or inside a kitchen cabinet.

JANUARY 3

" The deep pain that is felt at the death of every friendly soul arises from the feeling that there is in every individual something which is inexpressible, peculiar to him alone, and is, therefore, absolutely and irretrievably lost." – ARTHUR SCHOPENHAUER

Every single person is unique, so when someone we love dies, their mannerisms and idiosyncrasies are lost. They can never be replaced or re-created. There is massive grief in knowing and recognizing that the person you've lost can never return to you the same way they were present in life. It's okay to acknowledge these feelings and feel heartbroken that your loved one—with all their charms, oddities, and rituals—is gone.

JANUARY 4

MAKE a list of 10 to 15 things you loved about the person who died. This could be anything from "the cackling sound of her laugh" to "the way he always unfolded his napkin right when he sat down at the table." Then look for those traits and characteristics in the living people around you: family members, friends, and strangers. Of course, these people can't replace the person you've lost, but they can be small and meaningful reminders of your lost loved one's specialness.

"Do not sit still; start moving now. In the beginning, you may not go in the direction you want, but as long as you are moving, you are creating alternatives and possibilities." – RODOLFO COSTA

I often refer to life after loss as an "involuntary scavenger hunt." You didn't want to be on this mission of grief, but you're on it, so here you are, turning over rocks and trying on new rituals and testing out new paths to see which is the best fit for your new life after loss. It feels silly and disorienting at times, as if you're fumbling around a forest with no marked trail, but it's not the direction of your movement that matters at first; it's the fact that you keep moving, period. You didn't sign up for this life, but you have to live it. Creating momentum—no matter how slow you think you're moving—opens doorways to alternatives and possibilities for you.

JANUARY 6

PHYSICALLY moving is scientifically proven to boost mood and outlook. Try to walk for 20 minutes a day and see how moving your feet affects your grief. While you don't have to walk outside, fresh air is certainly a perk of walking, so try to get outdoors as often as you can. Grievers have told me that taking walks helps them get out of their heads; notice the small, quiet beauty of a blooming flower or a blue sky; and create the valuable illusion that they're "going somewhere" while grieving. To improve your walking experience even more, walk with a dog or a beloved human friend.

JANUARY 7

" Grief is a story that must be told, over
and over." — SALLIE TISDALE

We tell the story of our grief for two reasons: first, to solidify in our brains
and hearts that life without our loved one is our new reality; and second, to
realize that we are not alone. Just as grief is not a one-time event, telling the
story of our loss is not a one-time event, either. We must share the story of
what happened, to make sense of it for ourselves and to connect with others
who are experiencing similar pain.

JANUARY 8

FIND a place where you can tell the story of your grief with others
who are grieving. Two wonderful places to start are the Grief Recovery
Method (griefrecoverymethod.com) and the Compassionate Friends
(compassionatefriends.org). Additional support groups can often be found
at a local hospital, funeral home, or religious organization. The internet
also makes it possible to find loss-specific grief support groups, such as
those for the loss of a child, parent, or spouse; for loss in your 20s and 30s;
and for loss to suicide.

"In life, we make the best decisions we can with the information we have on hand." – AGNES KAMARA-UMUNNA

Losing someone we love can sometimes make us afraid of screwing up or making a mess of things in the future. Whether we're feeling guilty about the loss that happened or just scared of something bad happening again, analysis paralysis can accompany grief: "If I just had enough information, I could prevent feeling more pain." In reality, analysis has to stop at some point and a decision has to be made. Go easy on yourself when making difficult choices; you're doing the very best you can with all the tools and information at your disposal.

SOCIETAL convention says, "Don't make any major decisions within the first year of a loss," but in my humble opinion, that's hogwash. As much as we'd like to, we can't opt out of living because someone we love has died; sometimes life-changing decisions must be made immediately following a loss. If you have to make a big decision in the aftermath of loss, gather as much information as you can, call on friends and trusted advisers to help, and be sure you are as informed and prepared as you can possibly be.

JANUARY 11

" Once you had put the pieces back together, even though you may look intact, you were never quite the same as you'd been before the fall." – JODI PICOULT

The death of a loved one changes who we are at our core. While other losses are difficult and scary, they often impact only a few areas of our life (health, finances, work, romance, and so on). It's easy to compartmentalize such losses and remain more or less the same person we were pre-loss. But the death of someone we love rearranges everything about our "old self." We go from being somebody who has never seen, known, or experienced death to someone who comprehends death intimately. There is no going back from that; there's no unbecoming our new self.

JANUARY 12

IF you don't recognize who you are anymore, that's okay. Many grieving people report behaving differently after the death of a loved one, as if an entirely new person has come to live in their body. There's a lot of resentment involved in losing, practically overnight, who we used to be. Like, where did that kind, predictable, comfortable person go? If you're disturbed or distraught by your new self, gently speak to them as if meeting them for the first time. Say things like "We've never met before, so I'm curious to get to know you," or "I don't understand why you do the things you do, but I'm willing to learn," or "I know we're not meeting under the best of circumstances, so pardon me if I'm a little bitter and distant at first." You don't have to know or take ownership of your post-loss self just yet; you just have to acknowledge their presence.

" Resilience is not a fixed personality trait. It's a lifelong project." – SHERYL SANDBERG

While some people are born with a greater propensity for resilience, resilience is not a static characteristic. Resilience can be practiced, nourished, and built across your lifetime. If you feel like you're not bouncing back, well, you're in good company. The death of a loved one often marks the first time that people are forced to come back from something hard, scary, and life-changing. Each day that you are living beyond the day of your loss is another day you're building resilience. You're teaching your heart, mind, and body what it means to continue to live after the very worst has happened.

JANUARY 14

AS with building muscle in the gym, the results of your growth in grief won't be visible right away. Set a calendar reminder for six months from now, and on that date, check in with yourself and your grief. Ask yourself, "How have I grown since X date?" "What do I know now that I didn't know then?" "What have I seen, heard, experienced, or realized that I never saw, heard, experienced, or realized before?" Taking this resilience inventory helps you record and honor the small and large ways you're learning in your grief. For example, six months after my mom died, I graduated from college. It was the first major milestone I had to experience without her. I thought, "Six months ago, on the day of her death, I would never have believed I could graduate without her and not fall over dead from the agony of it. It was hard, but I'm still standing." This exercise is helpful both for acknowledging your accomplishments and for providing perspective on your ability to be resilient in the aftermath of loss.

JANUARY 15

"We all have to find our own ways to say good-bye." – SHERMAN ALEXIE

Friends, family, and society will tell you a lot about how you "should" say goodbye to the person you've lost. From memorial ceremonies to how long you're "allowed" to mourn, when someone we love dies, the people around us become unofficial grief experts. Annoying, isn't it? Don't let anyone tell you how to say goodbye. You and you alone are the expert on your grief and your relationship to the person who died. You have to find your own way to grieve the person you've lost and to honor, celebrate, and make sense of the fact that their life is now a memory. If the advice of a friend, family member, therapist, or stranger doesn't sit right with you, don't take it. Look for other people and spaces that validate the ways *you* want to say goodbye.

JANUARY 16

WE say goodbye in all sorts of ways, and for the loss of especially dear loved ones, we must say goodbye over and over and over again. If you're searching for ideas on how to say goodbye to the person you've lost, think of some things they loved or enjoyed in life. Did they like flowers? Plant a memory garden in their honor or schedule a date to walk around your local conservatory. Were they the family photographer? Compile a book of their photos or devote a wall in your home to pictures they took. Were they a lover of animals? Set up a recurring donation to an animal charity or volunteer your time at an animal shelter. With each action you take to say goodbye to your loved one, know that you're also saying hello to a new way of being alive without them physically here.

" Every broken heart has screamed at one time or another:
'Why can't you see who I truly am?' " – SHANNON L. ALDER

There is intense and immense heartbreak in the isolation of grief. Try as they might, the people around us never truly get it, and sometimes we even feel like strangers to ourselves. It's as if our hearts are screaming, "Why can't you see who I truly am?" We long to be understood and recognized in our grief. But more often than not, we sit frustrated and exhausted in the presence of those who will never truly "see" us. Take heart that this is a normal, built-in aspect of loss. You are not at fault for being unable to relay the full extent of your heartache, and your friends and family are not at fault for being uneducated when it comes to grief. There are communities of grievers the world over who have been in your shoes. Know that other grievers are out there, waiting to welcome you and your broken heart with open arms.

JANUARY 18

AT times when you feel unseen by the people around you, you can practice seeing yourself. On a piece of paper, write, "What do I feel right now that I wish somebody would just understand?" Allow your pain, rage, sorrow, and emptiness to pour out onto the page. If you're feeling nervous or guarded, remind yourself that this exercise is for your eyes only. When you've gotten all your feelings out, take a deep breath and write or say out loud, "I see you. I hear you. You're not crazy; you're just grieving. It makes sense that you would feel this way. I've got you. I love you." Practice this journaling exercise as often as you need. Yes, it's not fair that we have to be our own support system in grief, but sometimes only we can see and know exactly what we're going through.

JANUARY 19

"Death ends a life, not a relationship." – MITCH ALBOM

While their physical body is no longer here, your loved one lives on in your heart and mind. If history shows us anything, religious figures, celebrities, athletes, and other deceased figures are still alive in some way and worthy of receiving our continued communication and love. It's normal and natural for you to continue communicating with your loved one, even if they're not physically present to hear you.

JANUARY 20

WHEN my mom died, I kept seeing three-digit numbers with the same first and last digits: 212, 848, 393, and so on. I couldn't make sense of it at first, but I felt as if the numbers were following me around. Everywhere I looked, from bus routes to the hour given on digital clocks to my total at the grocery store, there were these little palindromic patterns. Finally, after a lot of irritated internet searching, I found a resource that proposed that palindromes were symbols of deceased parents "coming back" for a visit. 2-1-2 = M-O-M. I instantly got chills, and felt that these repeating numbers were my mom's way of attempting to continue a relationship with me after her death. Out loud, I asked, "Could you keep showing up this way? It makes sense to me now, and I'll know to look for you." Six years later, I still "see her" show up for me through palindromic numbers. What are some ways you can continue your relationship with your deceased loved one? Were they fond of birds, motorcycles, a particular song? You can communicate with them in the wake of their death by saying hello each time these signs and symbols appear.

" It is a curious thing, the death of a loved one . . .
It is like walking up the stairs to your bedroom
in the dark, and thinking there is one more
stair than there is." – LEMONY SNICKET

There's a groundlessness in life after loss, as if somebody is pulling the rug out from under you again and again. It's hard to find anything stable and secure to stand on, and when you do, there's always the fear that it's going to be taken away. Know that this sense of not having legs to stand on is completely normal and is a very real sensation brought on by loss. It's not pleasant by any means—in fact, it can be downright terrifying—but it is an expected part of grief.

JANUARY 22

FEELING safe in the world again becomes supremely important in the aftermath of loss. Try making a list of people, places, pets, songs, activities, and practices that help you feel secure and grounded. When you're feeling groundless or uncertain, choose an item from your list to engage with. Observe how it anchors you. Then rinse and repeat as needed. Know that what felt safe and secure before your loss may not feel safe and secure now, and vice versa. In other words, people, places, pets, songs, and activities that brought you peace of mind before your loss may no longer be comforting after your loss, and you might find yourself drawn toward stimuli you wouldn't have considered comforting before your loved one died. If you're looking for grounding resources, try asking friends, family, or your local mental health professional what roots them in uncertain times.

JANUARY 23

"Grief is perhaps an unknown territory for you. You might feel both helpless and hopeless without a sense of a 'map' for the journey. Confusion is the hallmark of a transition. To rebuild both your inner and outer world is a major project." – ANNE GRANT

Grief requires an entire restructuring of life, and that restructuring requires time, energy, focus, and perspective. It's a major undertaking, and it's normal for grief to consume much of your thoughts as you figure out how to "do life" without your lost loved one. Confusion, distraction, and forgetfulness are common. You're reorienting yourself to a world where your loved one has died, and that's a lot like using a compass that's gone haywire. You may find yourself moving forward just to be in motion, or you might head in a certain direction only to find that you don't want to go down that road. Allow yourself to make mistakes as you get your bearings again.

JANUARY 24

WHEN you feel confused, forgetful, overwhelmed, or like you're only going in circles, give yourself grace and mercy. Think about all the tasks you do in a day and add "while grieving" to the end of each. For example, "I drove my kids to school . . . while grieving," or "I sat through a two-hour meeting . . . while grieving." Looking at your everyday to-dos through the lens of grieving helps remind you that you are doing everything you used to do before your loss occurred *and* now you've got big, unavoidable grief in the mix, too. So, when you accidentally put your keys in the freezer, you can let yourself off the hook: "I misplaced my keys . . . while grieving."

" The goal is not to win but to open up. **"**

— BRIAN L. WEISS

Contrary to many societal teachings, there is no conquering grief. It's impossible to "win" at an emotional experience like loss, because grief is not that kind of game. The object of grief is not to make the grief go away, but to expand your heart to make room for it. When you live with an expanded heart, there is room for you and your grief to exist side by side.

JANUARY 26

WHILE there is much to be gained from movies and television shows with a strong grief slant, you might consider putting a ban on "grief TV" for a period. The media often wrap up grief stories in 90 minutes or less, with a pretty bow and a happy ending, but that kind of messaging subconsciously pressures us to find our own happy ending in grief. Remind yourself that triumph stories aren't real life, and know that grief in real life lasts a lot longer and is a lot more complicated.

JANUARY 27

"Grief is never something you get over. You don't wake up one morning and say, 'I've conquered that; now I'm moving on.' It's something that walks beside you every day. And if you can learn how to manage it and honour the person that you miss, you can take something that is incredibly sad and have some form of positivity." — TERRI IRWIN

I remind my clients over and over again that there is no definitive fix for grief. This may sound pessimistic or hopeless, but when you give up the hope that grief is meant to be solved, you embrace the reality that grief is meant to be experienced. In releasing the pressure to solve grief, you give yourself permission to experience grief, including all its ups and downs. You might find yourself smiling at a memory or looking for signs from a loved one, and those small joys get integrated into the larger, rich picture of your life after loss.

JANUARY 28

PICTURE grief as a real-life person walking beside you, and try speaking to it as you would speak to a friend. If you're feeling artistic or creative, you might even draw a picture of what grief looks like to you. For me, grief is a gray, ghostly figure dragging chains attached to its wrists and ankles. It always hovers close by, never too far out of reach. Some days, I'm angry at it and say, "I really wish you would disappear for a while!" Other days, I recognize that it keeps my mom's memory close by, and I thank it: "I forgot about the time she took me to see that play. Thank you for reminding me." You might discover that grief is not always threatening or bad, just present.

"We all have gifts to give during death . . . When all these gifts come together, they form a bigger picture. All these pieces, all these gifts connect during death and create some fuzzy mosaic, some living remembrance of celebration – the best of all possible remembrances – of what the deceased stood for, what and who the deceased loved, and what the deceased meant." – CALEB WILDE

We don't get through loss without taking some pieces of our loved one with us. Whether you physically look like your loved one or you picked up their habits, daily routines, or family traditions, we carry on living with fragments of our loved one folded into the person we are. What pieces of you are shaped by who your loved one was in life?

IN some ways, we get to choose what pieces of our loved ones we'd like to carry with us. Write down some things you adored about the person you lost. Did you like the smell of their perfume or cologne? Did you admire their warm attitude toward strangers? Did you appreciate their taste in music? Then brainstorm ways you can take some of these characteristics forward with you: for example, buying a bottle of their perfume/cologne to have on hand, greeting strangers warmly, or going to a concert by one of their favorite bands.

JANUARY 31

" Your loss is not a test, a lesson, something to handle, a gift, or a blessing. Loss is simply what happens to you in life. Meaning is what you make happen." – DAVID KESSLER

People will tell you all kinds of stories about what your loss means and where your loved one is now: "Don't cry! They're in Heaven," "Look at the bright side—you'll be stronger for this," "At least they're out of pain now." Don't believe any of them. Only you can decide what your loss means and where your loved one is now, if anywhere at all. Meaning and purpose are up to you to decide—and don't let anybody tell you otherwise.

FEBRUARY 1

SOME people find meaning from their loss right away, but most grievers develop meaning over time, as they continue to live more life and incorporate the loss into their overall story. If you're struggling to determine what your loss means or find yourself putting pressure on yourself to figure it out, try using the word *maybe* to soften the overwhelming permanence of meaning. For example, "Maybe her death helps me connect to others who have lost," "Maybe his dying is a sign that I should go back to school," "Maybe this means nothing at all." Treat each meaning statement as a piece of clothing you're trying on. Test-drive it for a while and ask yourself, "What would my life look like if I believed this meaning statement to be true?" Eventually, you'll find the meanings that resonate with you and the ones you'd rather leave behind.

"Courage doesn't always roar. Sometimes courage is the little voice at the end of the day that says, "I will try again tomorrow." – MARY ANNE RADMACHER

In grief, the best measure of your strength is not whether you're winning the battle, but whether you're standing up every time you fall. Sometimes after loss, we give life all we've got and still feel like we've failed. At the end of the day, we feel weary and alone. But who we are at the end of the day is not who we are forever. With each new day that dawns, we have the opportunity to try again.

NIGHTTIME is a hard time for grief. For most grievers, the dishes are done, the curtains are drawn, and the computer has been powered down. In these quiet, end-of-the-day moments, loss has an opportunity to crash right to the forefront of our minds and take over our thoughts. If you find yourself plagued by a bad case of the nighttime blues, consider making a "dance it out" playlist on your phone or putting on one of your favorite albums. (My go-to artists are the twangy all-girl group The Chicks; the gorgeous, ethereal three-sister band Joseph; and the jazzy Vince Guaraldi Trio.) Move and dance your way through the nighttime blues. Don't worry about looking good; this is all about redirecting your brain's attention to your body and moving the energy of grief out through music.

FEBRUARY 4

"Tears have always been easier to shed than explain." – MARTY RUBIN

Tears come from an illogical place—that is to say, tears are not the language of our heads; tears are the language of our hearts. Allow yourself to release the need to have a "why" for crying. It can be frustrating not to have a pinpointed source for your tears, but sometimes the answer is simply "grief" or "I miss my loved one." And that's worth crying about over and over and over again.

FEBRUARY 5

ONE enormous misconception that grievers have with regard to tears is "Once I start crying, I won't be able to stop," but I'm here to remind you that that is physiologically impossible. When I was training to become a Grief Recovery Specialist®, my instructor said, "Nobody cries forever," and a lightbulb went off in my mind. Realizing that it was not possible for me to cry and cry forever (filling up the room like that scene in *Alice's Adventures in Wonderland*), I was able to give myself permission to cry. The next time you feel that pressing lump in the back of your throat, tell yourself, "It's okay to cry, because nobody cries forever. There will be an end to this." See if that gives you the permission you need to release the tears you're holding back.

"A friend who says, 'I don't know what to say, but I'm here,' offers a live connection; a friend who is mysteriously absent is an additional drain on a person who can ill afford more sorrow." – JANET REICH ELSBACH

Grief complicates friendships like nothing else. Keep an eye out for friends who stand by you or show up virtually via text, call, or email on hard days. These are the people you want close to you in the aftermath of loss. They may not have anything comforting to say, but they are present, and that matters a lot when you're grieving. Go easy at first on friends who disappear or who are awkward about the death of your loved one. They have likely never been taught anything about grief, or have never been through it themselves. Allow them to drift away as you allow your other friends to take care of you. When the timing feels right, and if you're emotionally up for it, reach out and try to reconnect. You may be surprised by what you learn.

PICK out a greeting card with a pattern or drawing you love and write a kind, funny, or thoughtful note to a friend. Connecting with others helps us feel more connected to ourselves, and the physical action of writing a note can help our brain focus on a singular task. (Plus, who doesn't love getting a piece of snail mail these days?) If you're stuck for prompts, consider thanking your friend for being the funeral guestbook supervisor or for bringing up the recycling bins last week; telling a story about a photo of your loved one enclosed with the card; or complimenting your friend on something your loved one would have noticed about them.

FEBRUARY 8

" Grief is not just 'looking backward.' **"** – KATE BOWLER

There's a misconception that grief is about "looking backward," mourning someone whose life has been reduced to memories. But grief is also about "looking forward," realizing and grieving all the future events that your loved one will never get to participate in. Grief is half about mourning the past that was and half about mourning the future that never will be. You're not weird or crazy for jumping months, years, or decades ahead to envision a life without your loved one present. In fact, when loss happens, we often feel like we're losing everything all at once—past, present, and future. Sometimes in these moments, it's comforting to know that while your loved one can no longer follow you into the future, your memories and love for them can.

FEBRUARY 9

ONE way to honor the death of your loved one while "looking forward" is to ponder how *you* would like to die. Looking at the way another person died helps us piece together how we would like our own deaths to go. Create a will, consulting a lawyer who specializes in end-of-life matters or a local death doula to get help brainstorming your final wishes. Ask yourself, "If I had the ideal death, how would I like it to go?" Would you like to be an organ or body donor? Would you like to donate money, clothing, jewelry, or land to a charity? Would you like to be buried, cremated, or something else? Would you like a formal ceremony or a casual affair? What happens to your children, pets, and property? One of the very best gifts that can come from losing someone is the certainty you give the people in your life about how *you* would like to die and be remembered.

" We don't lose our memories by living well after loss." – CHRISTINA RASMUSSEN

A few of my clients have told me they're afraid to move on after a loss because they'll lose the treasured memories they have of their loved one. There's a false illusion that we can *either* step into a future that is vibrant and joyful *or* we can continue to grieve. In reality, both are true. We can have a future that is a beautiful blend *both* of our loved one's memories *and* of our desire to be happy, whole, and joyful again. Living well does not mean throwing away the person who died.

USE your imagination or an online word generator to make a list of 52 random words. Here are five to get you started: *breakfast, flower, school, table, music*. Once a week, choose a word from your list of random words and call forth a memory based on that word. For example, the word *breakfast* reminds me of my mom making cinnamon toast and joking about how toast is a Midwest staple, whereas my father's breakfast of choice, biscuits, is an essential breakfast item in the American South. I can still see her mixing cinnamon and sugar together in a Tupperware container, to always have on hand in the pantry. This exercise helps you keep your memories of your loved one front and center as you continue to live your life into the future.

FEBRUARY 12

" In grief, after even the happiest of relationships, we go over things again and again." – LAURIE GRAHAM

Rumination is a normal part of grief. Sometimes, thinking about a memory or an event over and over again can be scary, because our brains have never focused on something so intensely before. But setting a memory or event on repeat is our brain's way of solidifying the story and tying it to other stories and memories in our minds.

FEBRUARY 13

IF rumination is keeping you up at night, try practicing good sleep hygiene and creating a sleep schedule to acclimate your brain to a routine that powers you down. Drink caffeine-free herbal tea, take a bath, darken your bedroom, turn on a sound machine, and decrease the temperature of the room to help transition your mind from the hamster wheel of rumination into a restful state. You might even try a meditation app or podcast to help lull you to sleep. The best gift I ever received after my mom's death was a weighted blanket, which (like those weighted thunderstorm jackets for dogs) helped me feel safe, secure, and ready to rest.

FEBRUARY 14

" You will live in me always. Your words, your heart, your soul are all part of me. My heart is full of your memories. Thank you for the gift of your life. I will never forget you." — AMY ELDON

There are some things that remain true across time. We will always love the person we lost. We will always carry them with us. We will always be full of the memories we made with them. On this day that celebrates love and relationships, know that these foundational truths can never be taken away from you. They are the lifetime commitment that grief makes to us in our heartbreak.

FEBRUARY 15

WE can often produce feelings of love for ourselves when we do something loving for someone else. Celebrate the life of your loved one by volunteering at a local shelter; gifting a piece of your loved one's clothing, jewelry, or book collection to someone who would appreciate it; or donating to a charity they would have supported. Play your part in continuing your loved one's life by becoming a living channel for their love. Use your eyes, ears, hands, and mouth to become a messenger through which their love travels. How would your loved one want to show proof of their love in the world? You can make that happen.

FEBRUARY 16

"I know now that we never get over great losses;
we absorb them, and they carve us into different,
often kinder, creatures." – GAIL CALDWELL

Grieving your own loss opens you up to noticing and empathizing with the losses of others. Whether they talk about it or not, everyone you know and everyone you don't know is facing some kind of struggle. It may not be the loss of a loved one, but just like your struggle, it is hard, challenging, and changing their lives. It's difficult to picture grief as a gift-giving experience, but one gift of grief is the ability to recognize and honor the losses and hardships of others.

FEBRUARY 17

STUDIES show that doing something kind for another person can actually improve our mood. Hold a door for someone, give a compliment or a warm hello, or let someone cut in front of you in line. See how it feels to perform an act of kindness for someone else. Picture the recipient of your kindness as your loved one and imagine them with a grateful smile on their face.

"Acceptance is not a relief; it's the realization that you will always carry grief with you." – MARI ANDREW

We're taught that getting to a place of acceptance means having no more grief and holding no more negative feelings about the death of our loved one. In reality, acceptance is simply acknowledging that what happened did in fact happen and recognizing the bitter truth that death is permanent and irreversible. Acceptance isn't relief; it is the wholehearted realization that your loss happened and that grief is sticking around for the long haul.

CURATE your social media feed to include posts and images from people who are carrying their grief into the future with them. A host of therapists, celebrities, authors, teachers, religious leaders, and public figures have survived the death of a loved one and continue to honor their loved one through life. Consider these other grievers role models for accepting what has happened and also that grief goes on. Some of my favorite public figures to follow are Oprah Winfrey, who lost her beloved friend Maya Angelou; Mari Andrew, who lost her father; and Elizabeth Gilbert, who lost her partner, Rayya Elias. If you're not big on social media, try curating the magazines you read, the radio programs you listen to, and the email newsletters you're subscribed to. As much as you possibly can, make everything you consume in the aftermath of loss work for your healing, not against it.

FEBRUARY 20

"And one has to understand that braveness is not the absence of fear but rather the strength to keep on going forward despite the fear." – PAULO COELHO

Grief means being both brave and fearful. There is much to be afraid of in life after loss, and there is also an enormous amount of strength in the act of carrying on each day. You may not see it right now, but I assure you, everyone I've encountered who's grieved has had a moment six months, one year, five years after their loss occurred when they looked back and thought, "Wow. I can't believe I survived that. I can't believe I made it here." In that flash of realization, they acknowledge both the very real fear of life after a loved one dies and the tremendous courage it takes to continue living each day with that fear in tow. I know you'll have this moment one day, too, when you'll honor your fear and your incredible resilience together.

FEBRUARY 21

TRY thinking of fear as a backpack with straps permanently glued to your shoulders. In a journal or notebook write, "The fear I'm carrying today is [insert fears]." List as many fears as you like: for example, "the fear of forgetting my loved one" or "the fear that my life will always look like this." Once you've listed all your fears for the day, write at the bottom, "And I am choosing to show bravery by [insert actions]." Then list all the ways you're going forward despite the fear on your back: for example, "going to work," "attending my first grief support group," or even simply "getting out of bed." By visualizing fear as a constant companion, you give yourself permission to walk through each day with strength in every step. Fear and bravery are allowed to coexist.

" The bereaved need more than just the space to grieve the loss. They also need the space to grieve the transition." — LYNDA CHELDELIN FELL

When we grieve, we are grieving more than just the person we've lost. We are also grieving the life we knew before and the person we used to be. With a loved one's death, we step into a liminal space—we've stopped living our old life, but we've not yet stepped into our new one. And being in that transitional in-between is worth grieving. If you're in this space, give yourself grace and mercy. Everyone who has ever grieved has been exactly where you are right now. Everyone has had to grieve their own transition.

FEBRUARY 23

THREE powerful phrases—"right now," "in this moment," and "for the time being"—added onto any spoken or thought sentences let the people around you know you're in a state of transition, and that you're doing the best you can. For example, "I'm not ready to clean out Mom's house" sounds final, as if you might never clean out your mother's home. "I'm not ready to clean out Mom's house *right now*," lets both you and others know that this decision is where you are today and that you are open to cleaning out your mom's home in the future. Try using this tool when welcoming or turning away guests ("We're not accepting visitors *for the time being*"), making big decisions about your career ("*In this moment*, I'm comfortable going back to work"), and forming social plans ("I don't feel like going to tomorrow's fundraiser *right now*"). Knowing that you do not have to decide everything definitively today can help you feel like you have more room to breathe.

FEBRUARY 24

"You can't rush grief. It has its own timetable. All you can do is make sure there are lots of soft places around – beds, pillows, arms, laps." – PATTI DAVIS

It may feel silly or childish to surround yourself with comfortable objects after a loss, but for many grievers, being surrounded by comfort softens the mental, physical, and emotional blow of death. We can literally tuck and burrow ourselves into blankets and pillows or request to be hugged and held by someone we love. Of course, these objects are no replacement for the person we lost, but they can provide warmth, rest, and some measure of relaxation in the midst of a difficult season. Grief can't be rushed, but we can be snuggled into it for the ride.

FEBRUARY 25

IF you're struggling to determine what comforts you, think back to how you spent your time as a child. Did you love to draw, paint, or take pictures with a camera? Did you like to build things, bake, or dig in the dirt? Experiment with integrating a childhood pastime into your daily or weekly routine. See how you feel and continue the activity if it seems to help. Often what we gravitate toward when we're younger can help us process and express our grown-up troubles.

"Grief makes one hour ten." – WILLIAM SHAKESPEARE

Time is wonky in grief, and that's normal. Six months can disappear in the blink of an eye, and five minutes can drag on for what feels like decades. New events and experiences—of which there are quite a lot in grief—lend the illusion of both compressing time and extending it. If you find yourself forgetting what day it is, accidentally running late, or overbooking yourself, take heart; you're on "grief time."

FEBRUARY 27

IT'S normal to lose track of time when grieving. Set an alarm on your phone or computer for important meetings, events, and milestones. These alarms can be silent vibrations, dinging bells, or, if you're really tech-savvy, inspirational songs you love. You might even consider setting two alarms: one for the event you want to remember and another that goes off a day, a week, or a month in advance of that event. Allowing yourself time to prepare gives you a mental cushion of grace and leeway. You may not have needed to set alarms before your loss, but after loss, it's normal to be overwhelmed or forgetful. Think of alarm setting as a loving act in service of your future self.

FEBRUARY 28

"Promise me you'll always remember: You're braver than you believe, and stronger than you seem, and smarter than you think." — WINNIE-THE-POOH (A. A. MILNE)

Once, on a call with a client, I said, "You know more than you think you do." My client had just put words to a very real emotion, allowed herself to feel it, and generated actionable next steps for her grief based on that emotion—all with very minimal help from me. In that moment, I recognized that she, I, and so many other grieving people know far more than we think we do. Yes, we may be doing grief for the first time, but we are still capable and intuitive. We know more than we think we do.

FEBRUARY 29

ASK yourself, "If I could have anything in the world right now, what would it be?" Write down the first thing that comes to mind. For example, would you like an extra hour of sleep, or a hug from your loved one who died? Let your answer be far-reaching or impossible in this first step. Then take five minutes to brainstorm all the ways you could make your wish a reality—or as close to a reality as you can get. For instance, you might not be able to get an extra hour of sleep each night, but do you have time for a 20-minute nap in the afternoon? You might not be able to hold your loved one close, but can you visit with a friend or relative who knew them in life? You don't have to deny yourself comfort just because you can't obtain your "perfect vision" of support. Keep in mind, this exercise is not about "filling in" the hole left by loss; it's about providing scaffolding around that hole so it doesn't seem so big and empty.

" Some people believe holding on and hanging in
there are signs of great strength. However, there are
times when it takes much more strength to know
when to let go and then do it." – ANN LANDERS

Many grievers have told me they're afraid to let go because letting go means
forgetting their loved one. But that's not necessarily true. To me, letting go
means allowing yourself to release the white-knuckle grip you have on regrets
and missed opportunities, the guilt or shame you're carrying, or the pain in
your heart. It's impossible to forget your loss or the person you love who died—
and it would be ridiculous for anyone to ask that of you. It is possible, however,
to ease up on yourself in the self-torture department. Take a deep breath and
set yourself free. You cannot forget your loved one by letting go.

MARCH 2

WELL-MEANING friends and family will tell you to "just let it go," but
how can you? It seems impossible to just let go of the pain, the heartache, or
the memories of your loved one. So, instead of "let it go," try using "release."
Release comes from the Latin word *relaxare*, which means "to loosen, to free
from confinement and obligation"—and that can feel much clearer than "just
let it go." Ask yourself what you would like to loosen and free from confinement and obligation. Maybe you want to release the thoughts of your loved
one's final moments. Perhaps you want to release the obligation to chair
your neighborhood's block party this year. When you feel like you're holding
on too tight, finish this sentence: "Right now, I would like to release [insert
thing to be released]."

MARCH 3

"Become a possibilitarian. No matter how dark
things seem to be or actually are, raise your sights
and see the possibilities . . . always see them . . . for
they're always there." – NORMAN VINCENT PEALE

I will never ask you to be optimistic, but I will ask you to remember that
there is more to life than what you're experiencing right now. When death
happens, it seems like life will be dark and awful and upside-down forever.
In reality, though, it is only a season of your life. There is more than the life
you are living right now. You don't have to be hopeful, but it can help you to
remember that your future is full of possibility. Your life isn't over—just *life
as you knew it*. So, grieve, grieve, grieve, and know that something else is
always heading your way.

MARCH 4

MY clients often tell me they are filled with anxiety after the death of a loved
one. Now that they've experienced loss, it seems like a whole world of negative
possibilities has opened up and they're just tensing for the next bad thing to
come their way. Now that death has happened, only bad things can happen
from here on out, right? The truth is that both good and bad things are just as
possible as they were pre-loss. Try this: for each negative or anxious "what if"
that crosses your mind, pair it with another, equally strong *positive* "what if."
For instance, "My mom just died; maybe my dad is next" *and* "My mom just
died; maybe my dad will live to be a hundred." The goal here is not to eliminate
your anxiety or the voice asking "what if" but to remind yourself that there are
many possibilities in the future, and they're not all bad.

YOUR GRIEF, YOUR WAY

" We all want to do something to mitigate the pain of loss or to turn grief into something positive, to find a silver lining in the clouds. But I believe there is real value in just standing there, being still, being sad." – JOHN GREEN

We live in a world that tells us sadness is a pointless, useless emotion. There's visible and invisible pressure to do something with sadness so that it's not sad anymore. But sadness doesn't need to be alchemized into action or positivity right away. Sometimes it's okay to just sit with and feel your sadness, free from the obligation to make it something else. Sadness is a healthy, more-than-normal response to losing someone you love. So, let yourself have your sadness, freed from the pressure to transmute it. Know that sadness, just like every other human emotion, will pass.

SPEAK to yourself as if you are talking to a dear friend or to a child who is grieving. You wouldn't ask a friend or child to stop crying over the death of a loved one or to rush to find a silver lining in the face of loss. What would you say instead? Some of my favorite phrases to use on myself when I'm sad are, "Oh honey, of course you're devastated. I'm here" and "It's okay that you're sad right now. You don't need to be anything else." See how these phrases feel to you—or make up your own! It might feel ridiculous at first to speak to yourself in this way, but it's a marvelous practice in self-compassion and truly "seeing" your whole self when you're feeling a less-than-positive emotion. You are worthy of love and compassion—even more so in your sadness.

MARCH 7

"Grieving is a journey that teaches us how to love in a new way now that our loved one is no longer with us. Consciously remembering those who have died is the key that opens the hearts, that allows us to love them in new ways." – TOM ATTIG

I can hear you already: "But I don't *want* to learn to love my loved one in a new way!" It's normal to resist and reject the fact that death forces us to express our love for our loved ones differently. The good news is that our love never dies. We are just as full of love for our loved one as we were pre-loss, if not even fuller. We just have to determine where that love goes now that we can no longer physically be with our loved one. Everyone who has ever grieved has been where you are, asking, "Where do I put my love now?" The answer is unique for each person, and it's okay if that answer doesn't appear right away. Keep your heart open to new ways of expressing your love, knowing there are all kinds of ways love lives on after loss.

MARCH 8

ONE way to love your loved one in a new way after loss is to develop a ritual in their honor. Rituals can be as private as lighting a candle in your bedroom each morning or as public as running a 5K each year in your loved one's honor. As you move through your life after loss, keep your ears pricked for ritual ideas and inspiration from others. When you stumble upon a ritual that resonates with you, try it on for a while and see if it helps you feel connected to your loved one. If it does, wonderful. Carry on! If it doesn't, keep searching. You will find or invent one that works for you.

" The weird, weird thing about devastating loss is that life actually goes on. When you're faced with a tragedy, a loss so huge that you have no idea how you can live through it, somehow, the world keeps turning, the seconds keep ticking." – JAMES PATTERSON

One of the most surreal and reassuring truths about grief is this: you don't have to figure out how to go on; life is already doing it for you. Many grievers treat "going on" like a puzzle or a problem to be solved, when, in all honesty, time, grief, and life are always marching forward. Ease up on the pressure to figure out how to move on; the world is already in motion. Instead, seek the support of fellow grievers who are learning to live in a world that continues to turn without their loved one. There are many to be found.

MARCH 10

IT can be overwhelming thinking about the future after a loved one dies. Try this: Survive for the next 60 seconds. That's right. Just try to make it through the next 60 seconds. When that feels easy, try making it through the next hour. When that feels easy, try making it from meal to meal—breakfast to lunch, lunch to dinner, dinner to breakfast. Eventually, you'll be able to make it through a whole day. Then, before you know it, a whole week will have gone by. When grief triggers arise, or if you're having a particularly difficult time, scale surviving back to 60 seconds again, then an hour, then between meals, and so on. Use this exercise to rein in a racing mind that's spiraling out into an unknown future. It can keep something as abstract and ongoing as time within boundaries you can count and comprehend.

MARCH 11

"We bereaved are not alone. We belong to the largest company in all the world – the company of those who have known suffering." – HELEN KELLER

On the outside, family, friends, and total strangers might seem to have their lives perfectly together. You may feel like you're the only one in the world experiencing heartache at the level you're feeling it. And in some ways, that's true. No one but you knows *exactly* what it's like to walk in your shoes and experience your loss. But, in other ways, every single person who has ever lived knows what it means to suffer. Everyone has lost, grieved, mourned, or been heartbroken at some level. And there is solidarity and comfort in that.

MARCH 12

PEOPLE around us often say things like "Let me know if there's anything I can do." Ask them to tell you a story of a time in their life when they faced loss or suffering. You can phrase your request a number of ways: "I can't think of any errands I need run right now, but could you tell me about a time when it felt like your world was ending?" "I've got everything covered here, but could you write me an email or a letter about something hard you've been through?" On the surface, this may seem like a surefire method for "doubling down" on sadness, but when you're grieving, which would you rather hear: platitudes and clichés about overcoming hard things or stories from people who have also experienced struggle? You might discover that some of the people closest to you have survived extraordinarily difficult circumstances. And knowing that *they've* survived might instill some hope in *you.*

"Any painful experience makes you see things differently." – AMY POEHLER

We don't have to *try* to learn from pain; we just do. And often, what we learn from the death of a loved one is a new or different way of seeing the world. If you've seen the world one way your whole life and then experienced the death of a loved one, it might feel scary or overwhelming to have your beliefs upended overnight. Grievers have expressed heartache over loss of faith, loss of positivity, and loss of trust, to name just a few. Know that these "secondary losses" normally accompany a great loss like a death. I've been where you are, and while it feels like the end of the world, it's not. It's the end of the world *as you knew it*. Another world, a world that honors and includes the death of your loved one, is waiting for you.

SECONDARY losses are all the things we lose in addition to our loved one that we often don't acknowledge. There are three categories of secondary loss: immediate (losses you experience right when your loved one dies); gradual (losses you experience over time); and unexpected (losses that seem to sneak up on you out of nowhere). On a sheet of paper, draw three columns and label them "Immediate," "Gradual," and "Unexpected." In each column, list secondary losses you've experienced. For example, an immediate loss might be "our morning routine." A gradual loss might be "my financial stability." An unexpected loss might be "my memory of an old family recipe." Writing it down, similar to speaking it out loud, can take away the heaviness of juggling these multiple griefs.

MARCH 15

"Grief can be a burden, but also an anchor. You get used to the weight, how it holds you in place." – SARAH DESSEN

Grief is very heavy, and that can be annoying, exhausting, or even painful. But grief is also a grounding anchor of sorts, holding you to a specific spot on the time line of your life. There is a new sense of depth to your life now, brought on by the loss of a loved one, and that depth can never be taken away from you. You will always carry grief with you, and there is something weirdly comforting in its constant presence. With time and continued practice, you can learn how to live life with grief, moving forward while it keeps you connected to the moment your loved one died. There is room for both you and grief in your life.

MARCH 16

MANY of my clients tell me they feel their grief has absolute power over them. They use words like *paralyzing, crippling,* and *crushing* to describe the weight of grief. I encourage them to reclaim their power by speaking back to grief as if it were a living, breathing person. Talking back to grief can help you feel like you're building a relationship with grief as opposed to being totally pulverized by it. The next time grief shows up in your life, think or say out loud, "Hey, I thought I might find you here," or "Wow, long time no see! What has it been, five minutes, since you last showed up?" or "I'm having a little trouble breathing. Do you think you could scoot to the left just a smidge?" Speaking to and even joking with grief can discharge some of its all-consuming power and help you feel like you have a voice in how grief shows up.

" We must let go of the life we have planned, so as to accept the one that is waiting for us." – JOSEPH CAMPBELL

Grieving the person we lost is about so much more than mourning the life they lived. We must also grieve the path we were on before—the life we can no longer live as a result of our loved one's death. Releasing hopes and dreams is painful, but doing so allows us to make room for the life that is waiting for us. Our old plans and expectations were important and worthwhile, yes, but a future just as worthy of our hope and investment is coming.

MARCH 18

A lot of grievers feel pressure to untether themselves from their old life all at once, like ripping off a Band-Aid quickly to decrease the duration of the pain. But letting go all at once can feel massively overwhelming and, frankly, isn't really possible. Give yourself permission to let go of your old life in pieces. Whenever you're thinking about an element of your old life that is no longer present, name it out loud. For example, "I'm letting go of my dream of going back to grad school." In the next breath, name something true about the life you're living now. For example, "I'm living the reality that grad school is no longer a part of my plan and that I need to work full-time right now to make ends meet." Gradually, each truth you name will take the place of a former plan. As you release the pieces of your old life, you pick up pieces of your new one.

MARCH 19

" There are three needs of the griever: To find the words
for the loss, to say the words aloud and to know that
the words have been heard." – VICTORIA ALEXANDER

In order to give grief its rightful place in our lives, we need to be able to
define it, name it, and share our findings with others. Otherwise, grief is
this ambiguous, silent experience, a burden we shoulder alone. The grief stories of others are a marvelous place to find words to describe your loss. Once
you find the words, share them with a safe person or a community of safe
people. Other grievers will know why you need to say the words aloud and
will be more than willing to hold that space for you.

MARCH 20

IN the aftermath of my mom's loss, I struggled to read more than four or
five sentences at a time. Instead of dropping reading altogether—I love
books too much—I turned to the world of audiobooks. Somehow, listening
to words was easier than trying to read them, and I found peace and comfort in hearing another human's voice. Is there a book you've been meaning
to read but just can't seem to focus on? Try listening to it as an audiobook.
Platforms like Audible and Apple Books offer free trials to new members.
Don't want to pay for audiobooks? Libby is an app that allows you to check
out audiobooks from your local library. Also, many public libraries still have
audiobooks available in CD and cassette tape format. All you need to check
out an audiobook is a current library card.

"Grief and memory go together. After someone dies, that's what you're left with. And the memories are so slippery yet so rich." – MIKE MILLS

One of the most difficult realities of grief is that what's left of our loved ones—aside from any physical objects we choose to keep—lives only in our minds. Memories are all that we have of them, and because they are no longer alive, we don't get the chance to make new ones. We're left with a finite bank of moments to draw on. We can trigger these memories ourselves, but sometimes we'll find ourselves remembering a moment with our loved one when we least expect it. Fond memories of my mom come rushing back to me every time I hear the hymn "It Is Well with My Soul." Each time I hear that song, I feel as if a little treasure has been uncovered in my mind. In that moment, my mom is right there with me.

MARCH 22

SET a timer for 15 minutes. Close your eyes, take a few deep breaths, and picture a moment in your life before your loved one died. It could be a big milestone, like a wedding or a graduation, or an everyday memory, like a cookout or a drive to the grocery store. Really sink into that memory and feel your surroundings. What's the weather like? What do you smell, taste, and hear? Who else is around you? Picture your loved one interacting with you in the memory. Continue living in that memory until your timer goes off. When you return to the real world, remind yourself that you have this memory tool at your disposal at all times. You can visit memories in your mind, and each time you do, you train your brain to recall memories of your loved one with ease.

MARCH 23

"Don't let the perfect be the enemy of the good." – VOLTAIRE

Do you feel pressure to get grief right? You're not alone. With all the messages we receive about grief from friends, family, and the media, it's not unusual to think we should be doing grief in a certain way. Many grievers I know have unspoken rules that dictate how they're "supposed" to act, feel, and behave in any given moment—and it's just as exhausting as it sounds. Take reassurance in the truth that there is no one right way to "do grief" (and there's no such thing as a perfect griever). However you're doing grief right now is good; it doesn't have to be perfect. Don't let the pressure to be the *perfect* griever overwhelm your ability to be a *good* griever. Good is more than enough.

MARCH 24

IT'S beyond rare for anyone to pick up a new skill right away, and grief is no different. Enlist a trusted friend or family member to be your "good enough" coach and ask them to remind you, daily or weekly, that your best is good enough, no matter the task. Let them know that their job isn't to push you or motivate you; it's to remind you of your inherent goodness and the good job you've done as you live life after loss. Grief is the game, and your coach is your cheering section. If it helps, enlist more than one person to be your coach so that you're feeling extra supported during this time.

"Never compare your grief. You – and only you – walk your path." – NATHALIE HIMMELRICH

On the long road of grief, it's tempting to look over to the griever in the next lane to see how they're doing and compare yourself to them. It's human to want to know if you're making progress—and if you are, how much? How fast? How well? Take a breath and know that while there are similarities between grief stories, they can never be measured. Everyone feels their loss, their pain, and their recovery at 100 percent magnitude *for them*. Know that you have lots and lots of company on the long road of grief, but your path is not comparable to anyone else's—and their paths are not comparable to yours.

MARCH 26

GRIEF runs contrary to the glitz and glam of social media. While platforms like Facebook and Instagram are phenomenal for connecting grieving people, they also carry shiny, polished, idealized pictures of life after loss. Consider scheduling a screen-free day of the week, when you put down your phone and shut off your computer in favor of walking in nature or connecting with another human being in real life. Having a designated day away from technology will help you remember that other grievers' social media presence represents just one aspect of their lives; it's never the whole story. Just like you, every grieving person experiences the ebbs and flows of life after loss.

MARCH 27

"The most common way people give up their power is by thinking they don't have any." — ALICE WALKER

When my mom died, the type of grief I faced most often was some variation on powerlessness: hopelessness, helplessness, "resistance is futile." Because the feeling of powerlessness was so strong, I genuinely believed I did not have any control over anything; I thought I was a passenger of life, along for the ride. What I later realized is that I didn't have any power, control, or say in my *loss*, but I did have power, control, and a say in my *response* to my loss. Slowly, with practice and compassion, I learned how to *respond* to my loss by reclaiming my stake in my time, energy, and voice. I was not powerless, as I had initially believed, but power*ful*, just in a very different way from how I'd experienced power before.

MARCH 28

TAKING back our power is a lot more "micro" than "macro." It happens in the moments when we make small, sustainable shifts, not one colossal transformation—which is good for us, because every new day is another opportunity to reclaim our power. Try this: For 10 minutes a day, do something that honors your grief. Take a walk, write in a journal, meditate, make art, look at a piece of jewelry or a photo—anything, as long as it honors the fact that you are a grieving person living on Earth. Then go live the rest of your day. It may seem laughably small to spend only 10 minutes a day on your grief, but those 10 minutes—this 1 percent of your waking hours— represent a powerful, doable way to reclaim your power, choice, and freedom in the aftermath of loss.

"Grief seems at first to destroy not just all patterns, but also to destroy a belief that a pattern exists." – JULIAN BARNES

Structure and pattern dissolve after someone you love dies. If you feel like you're floating or don't have solid ground to stand on, you're not alone. At first, it feels like nothing will be solid ever again. That is normal. For most people, death is an experience that doesn't make sense, so it stands to reason that all the structures we use to make sense of things become one giant, meaningless blob for a while. If you're in this place, know that it is not forever; this disorienting initial effect of grief is not permanent. Eventually, as the days and weeks march on, you'll notice patterns returning. Structure and support will rematerialize under your feet. Give yourself grace to live in ambiguous "grief time," with the knowledge that you'll return to "Earth time" soon enough.

MARCH 30

WHEN life feels shaky or groundless, try using a totem to remind yourself that you are still here, grounded in the present. Some people carry a crystal or coin in their pocket. Others rub a favorite piece of jewelry. Your totem should be a physical item that goes with you everywhere—kind of like a security blanket for grief. Each time you hold on to it, know that you are alive, breathing, and grounded in the present moment. If it helps, try pairing your totem with a mindful phrase like "I'm here. I'm breathing. I'm present." I've seen grievers get memorial tattoos as totems, cut out pages from a beloved book to tuck into a wallet or purse, or have custom key chains made with gemstones or their loved one's initials. Your totem is a unique, special way to return to yourself when life gets overwhelming.

MARCH 31

" We can't be brave in the big world without at least one small safe space to work through our fears and falls." – BRENÉ BROWN

We all need somewhere to go when we're grieving. For as much as grief is a universal experience, the universe as a whole is not a safe space for grief. We need places that are kind and nonjudgmental, and secluded enough so that we can process the things that we're going through. It's normal to feel you need to hide away or shelter yourself before letting out big emotions or addressing major fears.

APRIL 1

GIVE yourself the gift of peace of mind by planning safe spaces in locations where you regularly go. For example, a safe space at work might be a stairwell or an empty office. A safe space at the grocery store might be your car in the parking lot. A safe space at the mall might be the candle store on the third floor. In a notebook or on your phone, plan out all the safe spaces you can go when your grief feels larger than life. Visit your safe space when you're overwhelmed or need to take a little break to compose yourself. If you're surrounded by others, offer a quick comment of reassurance: "I'll be right back; I just need to step away for a moment."

"The wound is the place where the Light enters you." – RUMI

Pain puts us in close contact with ourselves. When we are wounded by loss, we become vulnerable. It's in that place of helplessness and hopelessness that we are broken open enough to receive light—emotions like comfort, peace, and hope flow in alongside grief. It's as if loss shatters us so much that we have no choice but to experience heartbreak and hope simultaneously. Where we most hurt is exactly where we will best heal.

TRY this meditation before bed or during another time when you need to relax. Close your eyes and picture the wounds that grief has left you with. I've heard people describe grief as weights around their ankles, a hole blown straight through their chest, or a knife sticking hard in their stomach. Where is grief located for you? Find grief in your body and really feel the wound that the pain of loss has left. Take a deep breath. When you're ready, imagine a team of tiny helpers—these can be magical creatures like fairies or elves or real-life beings like a group of your loved ones or a flock of birds— going to work on your wounds. Imagine them applying ice, gauze, stitches, or ointments to the places that pain you the most. Allow yourself to be taken care of by these healing beings who bring their own sort of comforting light to your grief wounds.

APRIL 4

" When someone you love dies, you don't just lose them in the present or in the past. You lose the future you should have had, and might have had, with them. They are missing from all the life that was to be." – MEGAN DEVINE

There is so much more to grief than just death. In losing someone, you lose their presence in every single moment and milestone that appears after their death. Every hope, dream, and expectation you had for the future must now be reworked, because the person you love can no longer be there. It's normal to feel like you're grieving multiple losses when someone dies.

APRIL 5

IT'S easy to spiral into hopelessness thinking about a future that can no longer be. Every time a vision of the future without your loved one appears, take a deep breath, close your eyes, and feel the ground beneath your feet. Say to yourself or out loud, "It's true I will have to live a future without them. Right now, I am here in this moment." This helps you acknowledge the truth that your loved one cannot be there in the future and also grounds you in the present. Take four or five additional breaths if you need to while grounding.

"Accepting death doesn't mean you won't be devastated when someone you love dies. It means you will be able to focus on your grief, unburdened by bigger existential questions like 'Why do people die?' and 'Why is this happening to me?' Death isn't happening to you. Death is happening to us all." – CAITLIN DOUGHTY

Sometimes the loss of someone we love feels like a personal attack, as if God or the universe or some other force that's bigger and more powerful than us took our loved one away. Death feels like a ripping away, not a natural part of life. In all reality, death is happening to each and every one of us. We are all in the process of dying. When we reframe death as a built-in inevitability of life instead of punishment or pain coming from an outside source, we can find some small shred of acceptance.

APRIL 7

THE not-for-profit company Impermanence founded Death Cafe gatherings in 2011 as a way for people to discuss the very human experience of death. If traditional grief support groups aren't for you or you'd like additional support in grappling with the wholeness of death, consider finding a Death Cafe near you (deathcafe.com). In these relaxed in-person and online meetings, you'll probably meet fellow grievers, those in death care or similar professions, and people who have not lost a loved one but who are interested in learning more about death. Attending Death Cafes reminds me that I'm not the only one pondering the inevitable end of life and that many others have questions like mine. You may find that you have a similar experience.

APRIL 8

"Grief doesn't hit us in tidy phases and stages." – DR. JULIA SAMUEL

If you're expecting to grieve in a predictable or orderly way, this is your nudge to drop that expectation. While the media, ill-informed counselors, and misguided loved ones tout the linear model of Elisabeth Kübler-Ross's Five Stages of Grief, the reality is that the "stages" of grief are more like "buckets." It is super normal to oscillate among denial, anger, bargaining, depression, and acceptance—and also to experience emotions that don't fall into one of these five "buckets."

APRIL 9

MANY grieving people picture grief as a never-ending ocean voyage. Some days are stormy and overwhelming, with big swells that crash into their little boat and leave it with broken boards and them with bruises. Other days are sunny and still, with very little movement at all. Consider keeping a "captain's log" of your grief in a notebook or on your phone. Once or twice a day, set an alarm to check in with your grief and rank its severity from 1 to 10, 1 being "Smooth sailing" and 10 being "She's taking on water!" Remember, the purpose of this exercise is not to see an improvement in your numbers; it's to recognize that your grief is different every single day.

"Deep grief sometimes is almost like a specific location, a coordinate on a map of time. When you are standing in that forest of sorrow, you cannot imagine that you could ever find your way to a better place. But if someone can assure you that they themselves have stood in that same place, and now have moved on, sometimes this will bring hope." – ELIZABETH GILBERT

It's tempting to leap forward into the future and try to imagine what the Entire Rest of Your Life will look like now that loss has occurred. Other people have made it out alive; why shouldn't you? And exactly *how* are you going to get there? Take a deep breath and know that it's okay that you don't have all the answers right now. You don't even have to know the *how*; you just have to know the *that*—that one day you will be somewhere better than the forest of sorrow.

APRIL 11

SOLACE and a kind of companionship can be found in the stories of those who have gone before. Search your local library for books on grief and loss, especially memoirs by people you respect and admire. (Got a favorite celebrity? They've probably got a memoir published, and that memoir almost always contains a loss story or two.) If your grief won't let you concentrate on a book at the moment, explore podcasts, YouTube videos, and documentaries about loss. Each time you read or hear someone's story of recovery from loss, say to yourself, "One day, that will be me," or "I'll get to that place eventually." Take comfort in knowing that each storyteller has once been in your shoes.

APRIL 12

" In our culture I think most people think of grief as sadness, and that's certainly part of it, a large part of it, but there's also this thorniness, these edges that come out." – ANTHONY RAPP

Grief is never just sadness. Rage, anger, disappointment, and aggravation are normal parts of grief and can show up just as intensely as sadness and despair. It's okay to feel ripped off by loss or as if you had something taken away from you. It's also okay to be frustrated by family and friends who don't understand. You may additionally find yourself angry at God, the world, or even yourself. Allow yourself to be angry with the circumstances of your loss and the fact that it happened at all. You have a right to feel your feelings and express them. Know that anger, no matter how crazy or irrational it seems to your brain, makes perfect sense to your grieving heart.

APRIL 13

I once heard that "anger is a natural human response to injustice," and this quote was paramount in helping me express my anger. Once I stopped seeing anger as a crazy, inappropriate emotion that marked me as "bad" and saw it instead as just another way I expressed the injustice of my mother's death, I allowed myself to experience it. If you are able to do so, find a physical way to express your anger safely. I like playing loud music and screaming. Others shatter plates from a thrift store, hit a punching bag or pillow, or dance it out. Death is not fair, and it's cathartic to express our anger at death's unfairness in a way that doesn't harm ourselves or others. Let it out!

" There is no magic cure, no making it all go away forever.
There are only small steps upward; an easier day, an
unexpected laugh." – LAURIE HALSE ANDERSON

There are small moments of grace in life after loss. Take them when they
come, and acknowledge that receiving grace is a part of life after loss.
Contrary to what you may believe, these small moments of grace are not a
betrayal of your loved one's memory or a sign that things are about to get
worse again. You are allowed to experience sunshine every now and then;
it doesn't mean you've forgotten about the rain. These small breaths of
air—seeing something beautiful, enjoying a belly laugh at a joke, or really
noticing the sun on your face—are reminders that while grief is forever, it is
not all there is. There is room in your life for warmth and ease, too.

APRIL 15

ARE you willing and able to have a sense of humor about grief? There
are many hilarious outlets for grief. If you look hard enough, you can find
greeting cards, T-shirts, books, and pins that celebrate and poke fun at the
awkward, painful, and morbid aspects of grief. Some of my favorites are
Emily McDowell's series of Empathy Cards, Kate Manser's You Might Die
Tomorrow project, and Chantal King's line of Grieve Me Alone clothing and
merchandise. If you don't see a grief product that speaks to you, it's easier
than ever to make your own. Nothing says, "I'm grieving!" like a custom
coffee mug designed by you.

APRIL 16

"Language allows us to corral our experiences into story form." — MARK WOLYNN

Finding the words to describe our experience of grief feels like a full-body sigh of relief. When we're able to describe what we've been through, we can start to make sense of what happened. We can tell the story of our loss to ourselves and to others. We may not be able to knit grief perfectly into the old story of our lives, but we can use language to expand and integrate it into our life after loss.

APRIL 17

FREE writing can seem daunting at first. Staring at a blank page is not easy after a major loss. If you're not sure where to start writing about your loss, try corralling your experience into a haiku poem. The first line is five syllables, the second line is seven syllables, and the last line is five syllables. Usually, haiku are about nature, but in grief, the rules do not apply. Make your haiku about your loved one, your aching heart, or your relationship to grief. For example, "My heart misses Mom / Her arms and her hugs are home / I see her in dreams." Writing a haiku is a great way to get unstuck or give yourself a new way to write about your loss.

"The body remembers what the mind forgets." – JACOB LEVY MORENO

Do you find yourself getting tense or jittery when a big grief milestone appears? Do you have chest pains on the date your loved one died when it arrives every month? Do you notice yourself having more headaches, backaches, or aches and pains in general? You are not alone. Many people who have lost a loved one report "feeling the grief" in their bodies. Some eerily have the same symptoms their loved one had before death. Others experience unexplainable pains that come and go. It's normal to hold grief in the body after someone you love dies.

APRIL 19

CONSIDER seeing a doctor, chiropractor, nutritionist, acupuncturist, Reiki practitioner, or massage therapist about your body's various "grief pains." When you make an appointment, let them know you've suffered a loss recently and are feeling unwell. If they dismiss your pain or make you feel crazy, don't book the appointment and continue searching for another practitioner. If they take your grief pain seriously, make a complete list of your symptoms to discuss during your time together. Stay open to their suggestions for wellness and know that you are not the only one who's experienced physical pain after the death of a loved one.

APRIL 20

"Stop punishing yourself for being someone with a heart. You cannot protect yourself from suffering. To live is to grieve. You are not protecting yourself by shutting yourself off from the world. You are limiting yourself." — LEIGH BARDUGO

Society teaches us that it's not good to be the three -*ads*: mad, sad, or bad. If we express "negative" emotion, there must be something wrong with us, and we need to be fixed or silenced immediately. We can even turn this judgment in on ourselves and hate ourselves for feeling, even though our emotions are perfectly understandable. Expressing "negative" emotions doesn't make you bad; it makes you human. Give yourself grace and know that you are allowed to be a human with a heart.

APRIL 21

PRACTICE giving yourself permission to feel the full spectrum of human emotions, including feeling mad, sad, and bad. When friends and family say, "Just be strong!" "Your loved one wouldn't want you to feel bad," or "There, there. Don't cry," respond with something like this: "I know you're just trying to help, and you don't want to see me in pain, but [insert loved one's name] is dead, and some days that's still really hard for me." You can also turn this in on yourself and say something like "I know it doesn't feel good to experience the emotions of grief, but I do know I'm allowed to have them. My [insert relationship] is gone forever, and I have permission to feel bad about it." See if this gives you a little more breathing room when you're tempted to shut off your feelings.

" Those who contemplate the beauty of the earth find reserves of strength that will endure as long as life lasts. There is something infinitely healing in the repeated refrains of nature – the assurance that dawn comes after night, and spring after winter." – RACHEL CARSON

You may not believe it now, but your coming back is inevitable. Grief is not a linear slide into darkness. It is a cyclical path that eventually rotates into light. Spring comes after the cold, harsh winter. Yes, there are seasons when grief is louder and more disruptive, but there are also seasons when grief backs off, your strength returns, and night turns into morning.

APRIL 23

SIGN up for a class or activity you've been thinking about. If you don't have a class or activity in mind, get a recommendation from a friend or family member. Then show up for the class or activity. You don't have to stay for the duration, but stay at least for the first five minutes. If you can, try to meet one person you've never met before. Taking small risks like this is a wonderful way to prove to yourself that not all new experiences are bad and that you are capable of building a life that's filled with different experiences from the ones you're living now.

APRIL 24

" You will lose someone you can't live without, and your
heart will be badly broken, and the bad news is that
you never completely get over the loss of your beloved.
But this is also the good news. They live forever in your
broken heart that doesn't seal back up. And you come
through. It's like having a broken leg that never heals
perfectly – that still hurts when the weather gets cold,
but you learn to dance with the limp." – ANNE LAMOTT

Healing from grief is very similar to healing from a broken leg. You are never
exactly the same as you were before, and your life after must be modified to
accommodate the limp. Life after loss is not an impossible one to live, but
your activities, and your mindset, must shift to account for the new presence of grief. With time, focus, and self-forgiving practice, you can learn to
dance with a limp.

APRIL 25

IF you're feeling nervous about participating in an activity after loss, you
might find it helpful to offer yourself and the people around you a disclaimer. Telling your yoga instructor, "My dad passed away four weeks ago"
can help them meet you where you are skill- and ability-wise and help take
some performative "I'm doing fine!" pressure off you. Offering a disclaimer
is also a marvelous litmus test for whether spaces are welcoming of you as a
grieving person. If your disclaimer is not acknowledged or you're expected
to put your grief aside in order to participate, you might consider postponing
this activity or looking for a new activity that honors you in your grief.

"Nothing that grieves us can be called little: by the eternal laws of proportion a child's loss of a doll and a king's loss of a crown are events of the same size." – MARK TWAIN

There is no way to line two losses up side by side and say one is greater or lesser than the other. Each person feels their loss at 100 percent capacity for them within the context of their own life. Surrounding circumstances (age, race, income, sexuality, geographic location, cause of death, and relationship to the person who died) are woven into their loss story, but they cannot possibly determine the level of pain a person feels when someone they love dies. Avoid comparing losses and surrounding circumstances as much as you can. It may seem like someone has it easier than you do, but in the world of grief, there is no measuring.

APRIL 27

STORYTELLING is an ancient practice used to pass wisdom and pride from one generation to the next. What's one story about your loved one that you want the people around you to know? Write it down and mail it to a friend or family member or share it with them face-to-face. If you don't know where to start, tell a story about something your loved one taught you, share a silly moment you'll never forget, or highlight a milestone day in their life in detail (a wedding, a holiday, a graduation, and so forth). If you feel comfortable making your story more public, consider sharing it on social media and invite family and friends to share their own stories about your loved one.

" You start with a darkness to move through but sometimes the darkness moves through you." – DEAN YOUNG

At first, grief feels like this massive obstacle you have to conquer and overcome, as if it were the world's biggest and most intimidating mountain and you can see no way forward but to climb it. But sometimes in life after loss, the world's biggest and most intimidating mountain doesn't need to be climbed; sometimes grief just needs to move through us. When we experience grief in our bodies and our hearts, we don't have to try too hard to scale the mountain; grief is moving of its own accord. Sometimes, it's okay to ease up on the massive force we're channeling toward grief and allow grief to do a little bit of its own moving.

APRIL 29

FOR millennia, people have used dance and movement to move the energy of grief. They use their bodies to tell the story of what happened, how they're feeling about their loss, and what the experience of grief is like. Even if you're not a dancer, consider dancing as an outlet for your grief. Whether you shut the curtains and dance alone in your bedroom or join a structured movement class with others, releasing grief through the body helps unlock and move emotions you may not have words for. When you're feeling stuck or stalled, put on a song you love and dance it out!

" **When grief is deepest, words are fewest.**" — ANN VOSKAMP

We can talk about grief until we're blue in the face, but when it really comes down to it, grief is an emotional experience. Sometimes there just aren't words to describe the keen ache of loss, the specific pinprick of pain you're feeling. If you're struggling to come up with words to describe your feelings, it's okay. It's normal to feel first and find vocabulary for your feelings later. Allow your feelings to exist without the need to classify, define, or verbalize them.

MAY I

ENGLISH is not always the best language for expressing grief. Other languages have beautiful and clever words for expressing what seems inexpressible in grief. Try doing a Google search for "grief words from other languages." You might be surprised by what you find. Some of my favorites are *yūgen* (Japanese), "a profound sense of the beauty of the universe and the sad beauty of human suffering"; *saudade* (Portuguese), bittersweet longing or nostalgia for a person, place, or thing that is far away from you; and *Kummerspeck* (German), literally, "grief bacon," or eating that follows an emotional blow or season of sadness. Who knows? You might find exactly the word you're looking for.

MAY 2

" I ask not for a lighter burden, but broader shoulders." — JEWISH PROVERB

For as much as we'd like to live in a world free from loss, it's just not possible. We can't lighten the weight of grief by removing loss; instead, we practice ways to make the weight feel less heavy. We process grief in pieces, we share grief with friends and family, and yes, we exercise our grief muscles so that grief becomes more manageable to carry. We do what's humanly possible to live with loss.

MAY 3

SOMETIMES, recognizing the inevitability that grief will always exist can make it easier to bear. Because grief can't ever *really* go away, you can stop fighting it. Pretend grief is a permanent roommate and write a letter to it, acknowledging that it is a part of your life now. For example, "Dear Grief, I've learned that your stay here is forever, and to tell you the truth, I'm not happy about it. Life was a lot simpler before you came along. But I know I can't make you go away, so let's figure out a way to make this work. I've fixed you up a room in my heart. I'm sure Love and Compassion will make great housemates for you. This won't be easy, but I know we'll stay in touch. You can't stay quiet for long." Treating grief like an intrusive roommate instead of a relentless punishment can help you transition from fighting grief to integrating it into your life.

YOUR GRIEF, YOUR WAY

MAY 4

"New beginnings are often disguised as
painful endings." – LAO TZU

Death is an ending, but it is not *the end*. The day your loved one died marks
the beginning of a new life for you, a life where your loved one is no longer
present in the physical world. It's a horrendously painful ending, and simultaneously, it marks a new beginning for you. Their death is not the end of
your story as a whole, but the end of a very beautiful and important chapter
in your life. Your task in this new beginning is to grieve the painful ending—
and to learn how to navigate life in the aftermath of loss.

MAY 5

WHILE it's rarely advertised this way, grief is a mental health event.
Losing someone you love affects the way your brain functions. If you have
preexisting mental health challenges, loss may increase or change the way
your condition expresses itself. If you do not have preexisting mental health
challenges, loss may unlock conditions like anxiety and depression. They
may not be permanent, but they do affect your day-to-day life. Experiencing
changes in your thoughts, moods, and behaviors is a completely normal and
natural response to grief. A grief-friendly therapist can help you understand
how your brain has changed and, if necessary, offer you a formal diagnosis
or helpful medication. The most comprehensive search engine for therapists
is psychologytoday.com. Note that many practitioners are able to service
patients remotely (if you cannot find one in your area), and some practitioners even offer a sliding payment scale for their services. When shopping
for a therapist, ask if they have experience working with grief.

MAY 6

"Forgiveness means giving up all hope for a better past." — LILY TOMLIN

Just about everyone dies in the middle of a conversation. There are things left unsaid, actions unperformed, and fences not mended. Whether you need to forgive your loved one or yourself, know that forgiveness doesn't mean being okay with the way things turned out. It simply means that you stop beating yourself up for not being able to make things any different. In forgiveness, you allow yourself (or the other person) to be human.

MAY 7

MANY of my clients have an easier time forgiving others than forgiving themselves. If you're struggling to forgive yourself for something (whether it was something you did or said or something you *wish* you'd done or said), try this: Sit in a quiet place, put your hand over your heart, and say, "I forgive you for [insert action]." Then inhale and exhale three times, holding space in your mind for your humanness and self-love. If this is too "out there" for you, face yourself in a mirror and offer yourself forgiveness as if you were offering it to another person, or find a photo of yourself as a child or baby to forgive. Know that forgiveness is usually not a one-time event. It's a practice that is carried out over and over again. You may have to forgive yourself 12 or 20 or 200 times for something you didn't say or do. That's okay. Just take a deep breath and say, "I forgive you for [insert action]." Then inhale and exhale three times.

"Grief is a world you walk through skinned,
unshelled." – ARIEL LEVY

Someone once described grief to me as having all their skin turned inside
out, as if all their nerve endings were suddenly and mercilessly exposed
to the world. Everything feels more extreme and more dire with grief, as
if there's no way to stop the zaps of pain from coming. If this is your experience, know that you are not alone. So many grievers know just what it's
like to be living raw, as if every sound, smell, touch, taste, and sight were a
violent assault on their bodies.

MAY 9

IT'S tempting to want to numb out the world in the aftermath of loss.
Living in a world without your loved one is so painful that anything that
promises a respite from the agony—even if you've never considered it
before—suddenly becomes an option. Instead of reaching for drugs or
alcohol, consider engaging with a calming sensory experience. Ease your
nerves and the feeling of overexposure to the world with a warm bath, a
meal cooked and served slowly, or a quiet walk. See if you can identify the
things that stress you the most—Is it people? Loud noises? The endless news
cycle?—and find small ways to temporarily escape them. Creating these
pockets of calm away from the harsh world can help you feel less stressed
and that you have some bit of control over your grief experience.

MAY 10

"Grief is at once a public and a private experience. One's inner, inexpressible disruption cannot be fully realized in one's public persona." – MEGHAN O'ROURKE

One of the biggest tragedies of grief is the fact that its effects are largely invisible. As much as we try, we cannot make the people around us see or comprehend what we're going through. Grievers often describe themselves as "living in two different worlds" or "having two different selves." There's the persona we perform out in the world, and then there's the person we are behind safely closed doors. It makes sense that we can't be our full grieving selves in public, but it's also sad that some of the people closest to us have no idea what we're *really* going through.

MAY 11

MAKE a list of three to seven people who can be "safe zones" for you. These should be friends or family members whom you can confide in free from judgment or unsolicited advice. Often, these people either are two or three steps removed from the person who died or did not know the person who died at all, such as a therapist or a trusted coworker. (The grieving can't always comfort the grieving, unfortunately.) Let them know you think of them as a safe zone for you in this hard time, and ask them if they would be willing to be a recipient of texts, calls, video chats, or emails on especially hard days. Having a team of nonjudgmental human safe zones is crucial to feeling supported and seen in the aftermath of loss.

❝ I've learned that I still have a lot to learn.❞ – MAYA ANGELOU

Nothing humbles us like grief. I've yet to meet a grieving person who is also a know-it-all about grief. Grief puts us back at square one, back in elementary school, and we are practically forced to assume a beginner's mind and work through loss from the ground up. Remember that you are not supposed to know how to grieve before grief rolls into your life. You're doing it as you're doing it, and that's exactly how it should be. You still have a lot to learn, but so does everyone else who is grieving.

MAY 13

REMIND yourself daily that you are practicing grief. You are learning what it means to be a grieving person—and for that reason, you deserve mercy and second chances galore. Reframing grief as a lifetime skill-building process instead of a one-time mountain to climb does wonders for a grieving heart, especially if you, like me, have the tendency to "should" yourself to perfection. When you feel you've screwed up or made a mess of things when it comes to your grief, say (out loud or in your head), "I'm just practicing!" or "This is my first time grieving!" See if it helps you grant yourself space and time to learn.

MAY 14

"One often calms one's grief by recounting it."

— PIERRE CORNEILLE

You might think that reliving your grief story is only bringing up the past or staying stuck on the negative. In fact, the opposite is true. Research shows that retelling what happened can help us make meaning of our loved one's death, cope with the hole the loss has left, and locate others who understand what grief is like.

MAY 15

SEARCH meetup.com, Facebook Groups, or your local funeral homes, religious institutions, or hospice organizations to find communities of grievers you can share your story with. Many groups are loss-specific—you can find groups for the loss of a child, the loss of a spouse, loss to suicide, the loss of a sibling, and so on. If a loss exists, there is a group for it somewhere online or in person. In these safe community spaces, you can practice sharing your own loss story and hearing and holding space for the loss stories of others. Together, you can help one another uncover meaning, find new ways to cope, or express feelings you may not have been able to name alone. Feel free to "try it on" at first by entering an in-person or online group as an observer. If you like the conversations you hear happening, join a preexisting conversation. When you're feeling ready, start your own. There is room for you and your loss.

" Empathy is different from sympathy. Sympathy is standing on the outside of a situation and looking in (e.g., 'I'm sorry you're sad'). Empathy is stepping into the situation with the other person and feeling the emotion with them (e.g., 'Wow, this is sad')." – MICHAEL S. SORENSEN

There's a big difference between sympathy and empathy. Sympathy is standing at the top of a well shouting, "Sorry you fell in!" Empathy is going down the well, sitting next to the person at the bottom, and saying, "Wow, this is dark and damp. I can see how this is unpleasant for you." Maybe this is why so many grievers detest the phrase "Sorry for your loss." It feels like it's coming from the outside of a situation, because it is. Keep an eye out instead for the people in your life who acknowledge the pain and sadness of your loss. They are the ones who will sit next to you in your grief.

MAY 17

IF you find yourself in a conversation with a person who's trying to fix you or save you in your grief, you have a right to request empathy from them. If they say something like "Have you tried massage?" or "When are you going to start dating again?" take a deep breath and respond with something like this: "I know you're trying to help, because you see that I'm hurting, but it would be really helpful to me if you could acknowledge that I'm hurting first." If they are truly a good friend and support to you, they should be willing to make the switch. If they are not willing to pause and acknowledge your pain first, distance yourself from this person and look for others who will be more empathetic to you in your grief.

MAY 18

"The bereaved cannot communicate with the unbereaved." — IRIS MURDOCH

When we lose someone we love, we enter into a human experience that some of our closest friends and family cannot understand. We are on Planet Grief speaking the language of grief, and they are on Planet Earth speaking the language you spoke in your life before loss. Sometimes, getting the people around you to understand what it's like to grieve is kind of like getting a person who speaks another language to understand you. It can be frustrating and isolating. But there is hope in the form of other grievers. It's refreshing and relaxing to be in the presence of another person who just gets it. There's no explaining, no fumbling, and no trying to figure out the "right" way to say it. There is immediate understanding.

MAY 19

ONE way to commemorate a loved one who has died is to gather a collection of stories and photos of them in a scrapbook. A few months before a special anniversary (such as your loved one's birthday), send out a call to all your family and friends requesting photos and memories for a memory book. Be sure to provide parameters for storytelling (no crude language, 2,000 words or fewer, handwritten or email, and so on) and a date for when submissions should be delivered to you. On the anniversary, take a video or audio recording of yourself reminiscing with the finished scrapbook and send a copy to everyone who participated. Consider uploading the scrapbook to a digital file-saving program like Dropbox or iCloud, so others who knew your loved one can access the file forever.

❝ Grief, as I read somewhere once, is a lazy Susan. One day it is heavy and underwater, and the next day it spins and stops at loud and painful, and the next day at wounded keening, and the next day numbness, silence.❞ – ANNE LAMOTT

Grief is unpredictable, and that's exactly how it should be. If you feel like you're stuck on a roller coaster or caught up in an unnavigable storm, you are not alone. I often think of grief like a slot machine. Each day I wake up, the dials turn, the combinations of emotions and experiences go round and round, and the wheels stop at whatever strange combination I'm about to experience that day. No two grief days are alike . . . and that's normal.

MAY 21

IN addition to sharing your own story in a group setting, listening to the stories of others can help you feel less crazy in grief. Knowing that there are people out there who are on their own grief roller coasters can be comforting and reassuring. Use an app like Apple Podcasts, Spotify, or Google Podcasts to find podcasts (free, on-demand radio programs) about grief and loss. You can start with mine, which is called *Coming Back: Conversations on Life After Loss*. There are thousands, if not hundreds of thousands, of podcast episodes about continuing to live after a loved one has died, and hearing grievers tell their stories in their own words can give you a sense of "me too" unlike anything else.

" Regardless of the source of the rage, something
has to happen to recognize it, bless it, contain it,
and release it." – CLARISSA PINKOLA ESTÉS

We cannot let go of grief until we're able to see it, honor it, and define it—and
goodness knows that doesn't happen all at once. Life after loss is a continual
process of examining grief, giving it space to show up and to influence you,
and figuring out where to place it within the context of your life story. Only
then can you begin to release it. I don't say this to discourage you, but to give
you permission; you don't have to "do grief" all at once. In fact, you can't, and
that's more than okay.

MAY 23

CREATE an altar for your grief in your home. Whether or not you're
religious, an altar is a beautiful way to give grief and your loved one physical space in your day-to-day life. I've seen all kinds of altars, ranging from
the more traditional photo-and-a-candle-on-the-dresser type to an entire
room devoted to memorializing a loved one. No matter what form your altar
takes, it should remind you of your relationship with and your love for your
loved one every time you engage with it. Each time you pass by or enter into
this sacred altar space, remind yourself that part of grieving is making room
for grief to show up. Allowing grief space in your physical world helps you
process it in your mental, emotional, and spiritual world.

"Surrendering isn't about what you do, but who
you're being as you do it." – JEN SINCERO

What kind of griever do you want to be? Living life after loss isn't so much
about the actions you take to surrender to the grieving process as it is about
the person you are while you're surrendering. It's worth asking yourself: "If
this could go exactly the way I wanted it to, who would I be? How would I
behave? What would I believe to be true about myself, my loved one, others?"

MAY 25

ONE of my absolute favorite forms of self-care in grief is emotional validation. If you've never heard of emotional validation before, that's okay.
Basically, it's seeing yourself the way a compassionate outsider would see
you and saying, "I see you. I understand why you feel that way. I hear you." In
my opinion, the very best one-liner we can say to ourselves when we're grieving is, "I believe you." We spend so much time trying to prove our grief to
others or to display the pain in our hearts that simply acknowledging it with
the words "I believe you" can feel like an enormous sigh of relief. For example, if you say, "I'm exhausted," then respond, "I believe you." If you say, "I'm
so angry that he won't be here to help me raise the kids. I feel so ripped off,"
then respond, "I believe you." If you say, "I wish the last thing I said to her
was more profound," then respond, "I believe you." Validating your feelings
in this way can remind you that while you may have to get others to buy into
your grief experience, you always have your own back.

MAY 26

"You can't control what comes up, only how you respond." – DAN HARRIS

The death of a loved one is a glaring reminder that we are not in control of everything. There are some things in life that fall out of our jurisdiction, and death is one of them. We can't control the fact that we've lost someone we love; what we *can* control is how we respond to it.

MAY 27

TRIGGERS are a big pain point in the aftermath of loss. Usually formed unconsciously, these neutral stimuli (sights, sounds, smells, tastes, and sensations) can send you spinning to emotional places you'd rather not inhabit. At their worst, triggers manifest as PTSD and can really impede your everyday life. (If you believe your triggers have impacted your ability to work, sleep, or connect with others, search for a PTSD-trained therapist in your area.) If you're looking for a way to disconnect triggers from their neutral stimuli, try this: Next time you're faced with a trigger, do something totally kooky instead. For example, I used to zone out and cry when I saw the exits for Duke University Hospital on the interstate. (It's where my mom was treated and where my family and I spent the better part of four years.) A dear friend and mentor of mine suggested that I burst into song every time I had to drive by those signs. The first time I tried it, I felt ridiculous. But I didn't zone out and cry, and that was amazing to me. I thought I'd be locked into my trigger/response pattern for years. Now, seven years later, I don't always burst into song when I see the signs for Duke University Hospital, but I am most definitely singing in my head.

MAY 28

" Start by doing what's necessary; then do what's possible; and suddenly you are doing the impossible." – SAINT FRANCIS OF ASSISI

It's hard to live life after loss, because we don't forget what life before loss was like. We remember what we were capable of; we remember what we used to do; we even remember how much energy we had. And it's easy to shame ourselves into not doing enough when we can't be the people we used to be. Take a deep breath and remember that you have just lived through one of life's hardest and most devastating experiences, the death of a loved one. You cannot be who you were, at least not right away. Start by surviving, then shift your focus to thriving.

MAY 29

EAT foods that are grief-friendly. After the train of sympathy cakes, casseroles, and sculpted fruit leaves your house, stock up on nonperishable nourishing foods like soups, frozen veggies, beans, rice, and oatmeal. Having foods around that are wholesome and easy to prepare is key to feeding your body after loss. If you're experiencing anxiety or spinning thoughts after the death of a loved one, consider cutting back on caffeine, sugar, and alcohol for a while, especially before bed. This is not to say that you can't have treats in the house—my favorite is frosted breakfast cereal—but when your body is nourished, your head, heart, and spirit get nourished, too.

MAY 30

"Grief is in two parts. The first is loss. The second is the remaking of life." – ANNE ROIPHE

While grief can't be cleanly divided, I've noticed that grieving people generally describe two types of grief: grief for the loved one who's died and grief for the life before loss that has died. It's normal to feel like you're holding more than one funeral, especially if your loved one's death has drastically changed your life. It can seem like you're mourning not only the person you lost, but everything about your "life before" that you can never get back.

MAY 31

WHILE nothing can replace your lost loved one, many grievers report that taking care of a living thing after a loved one dies is healing and life-giving. Start small, with a potted plant or a seasonal blooming bush for your yard. If you feel ready to take on more, consider fostering or adopting a pet from your local shelter. Watching another living thing grow and change is a wonderful way to remind yourself that you are also growing and changing. While plants and animals aren't perfect mirrors for us, they can offer us hope, companionship, and love in their own ways.

" If you're worried that giving permission to experience and engage with emotion will turn you into something you're not or someone you don't want to become – it won't. It will, however, give you the opportunity to be your most authentic self. We are wired to be emotional beings. When that part of us is shut down, we're not whole." – BRENÉ BROWN

Sometimes it's hard to let grief in because we're afraid it will change us. In reality, we are already changed by grief. Expressing grief simply allows us to express more of who we already are. While you may think shutting yourself off to grief will help you heal, the opposite is true. Letting grief show up and have its say is the key to staying whole in the aftermath of loss.

JUNE 2

WRITE yourself a personal permission slip for grief. On a sheet of paper write, "I give you permission to feel [insert emotions]," "I give you permission to behave like [insert behaviors]," "I give you permission to cry whenever [insert triggers]." Sign your name at the bottom and hang your permission slip up somewhere where you'll see it every day. Each time you pass by it, remind yourself that you are the first and best person to give yourself the space and grace you need to experience grief.

JUNE 3

"Grief is a normal and natural response to loss. It is originally an unlearned feeling process. Keeping grief inside increases your pain." – ANNE GRANT

I love this framing of grief as "an unlearned feeling process." Allowing ourselves to be novices at grief helps us be more forgiving with ourselves as we learn not just what it means to grieve, but what it looks like specifically when *we* grieve. It also gives us a flexible kind of permission to express our grief any way that feels right to us. Traditional talk therapy and group support are the most common methods of grief support, but any way we express and process grief is appropriate.

JUNE 4

TRY taking grief out of the box and exploring art therapy, coloring, or painting to express your grief. Whether you identify as "creative" doesn't matter; no one will see or judge your work. Just start making marks on the page. You might like a more structured format, like coloring pages from grief artist Joanne Fink or a guided online art course from Project Grief. You may also like just setting aside a few moments per day to doodle or sketch out what you're feeling. If you're looking for a place to start, try drawing what you think grief looks like, outlining and coloring in a word that describes your grief, or painting something that made you smile today.

" 'You'll get over it . . . ' It's the clichés that cause the trouble. To lose someone you love is to alter your life for ever. You don't get over it because 'it' is the person you loved. The pain stops, there are new people, but the gap never closes. How could it? The particularness of someone who mattered enough to grieve over is not made anodyne by death. The hole in my heart is the shape of you and no-one else can fit. Why would I want them to?" – JEANETTE WINTERSON

"I want to get over my loss!" said no griever ever. We don't want to "get over" our loss because "getting over" our loss means "getting over" or forgetting our loved one. No, we want the opposite, in fact. We want to find ways to honor and memorialize our loved one so that we can learn to carry the hole that their death has left in our hearts and our lives. We want their life and their legacy to mean something—and making that meaning has nothing to do with "getting over it."

INVENT a special day that honors your loved one and their legacy. Did they love to bake? Host an annual cookie swap with friends and family. Did they obsess over a TV or movie franchise? Put together a screening day, complete with popcorn and costumes, and binge-watch it in full. Grieving well doesn't mean forgetting all about the person who died. It means integrating their memory and energy as best we can into the lives we are forced to live without them. Get creative! There is no wrong way to celebrate your loved one.

JUNE 7

" The greatest mistake you can make in life is to continually fear that you will make one." — ELBERT HUBBARD

In one of my online courses, I teach grieving people how to say goodbye to the myth of the perfect griever. We all think we should be a certain type of person in the aftermath of loss, but our expectation isn't always reality. Allow yourself to make mistakes in your life after loss and to let the pressure of being the perfect griever fall by the wayside. You are allowed to be new at this.

JUNE 8

SIGN up for a skills-based class you've never tried before. This could be something artsy, like embroidery, pottery, or printmaking, or something adventurous, like craft brewing, beekeeping, or sailing. No matter what class you sign up for, make sure there's a clear and identifiable goal at the end: throw a bowl on a wheel, make a block print, learn to use a compass, and so on. Even if your final product is not something you're proud of, you did it— and the world didn't end because it wasn't perfect! Learning a new skill (and being bad at it at first) helps you show yourself grace and maybe even a little humor, too, as you navigate the skill of learning to grieve. And who knows? You might just meet another grieving person.

"People in grief need someone to walk with them without judging them." – GAIL SHEEHY

Judgment is the death of trust, vulnerability, and openness. When others judge us in our grief, they consciously or unconsciously signal to us that they are not safe places for us to share everything we're thinking and feeling. It's natural in the aftermath of loss, as in life in general, to gravitate toward people who are nonjudgmental and receptive. We all need witnesses to our stories, especially when we lose someone we love.

JUNE 10

IT'S not easy to work grief into the everyday, which is why I absolutely love grief retreats and grief-themed vacations. Take grief off the grid and connect with others who are grieving by going on a retreat, doing a weekend workshop, or combining grief and the great outdoors. A simple online search for "grief retreat" or "grief vacation" will yield lots of results. My personal favorites are Camp the Dinner Party (Camp TDP), for 20- and 30-something grievers; Soaring Spirits International's Camp Widow, for widows of all genders; and the Grief Cruise, which welcomes anyone who has experienced the death of a loved one. In going on a grief retreat, not only do you get to connect with other grievers and shake up your routine, but you also receive the perspective and insight that travel often brings.

JUNE 11

" We all carry the dead with us everywhere we go. "
— CALEB WILDE

Whether you can see it or not, just about everyone you know is carrying
a dead person (or two) around with them. These dead loved ones aren't
in physical form, of course, but exist in stories, memories, clothing, and
jewelry. We are all made up of the people who came before us and the people
who died in our lifetimes. We all have a story about a dead person to share.

JUNE 12

IT'S perfectly normal to wear a piece of your loved one's clothing or jewelry to keep their memory close by. There is no right or wrong way to "wear"
your loved one. Some grievers save special pieces for big occasions; others
wear their mementos every single day. It's up to you how you'd like to honor
your loved one through their treasured wearables. Even smelling like your
loved one via perfume or cologne is acceptable! The day after my mom died,
I snuck into my parents' bedroom and pilfered her scented everyday lotion
from the top of her dresser. I still dab it on my wrist on days when I need a
boost of confidence.

" Every one of us will go through things that destroy our inner compass and pull meaning out from under us. Everyone who does not die young will go through some sort of spiritual crisis, where we have lost our sense of what is right and wrong, possible and impossible, real and not real. Never underestimate how frightening, angering, confusing, devastating it is to be in that place. Making meaning of what is meaningless is hard work." – KERRY EGAN

No one can tell you what your grief means. You are the only person who decides what meaning, if any, should be assigned to the death of your loved one. While well-meaning friends and family will have their own interpretations of the role of loss in your life, it is up to you and only you to decide what it all means.

JUNE 14

MANY grieving people make meaning of their loss by giving back to their communities. Consider donating blood or plasma, doing volunteer work, or contributing financially or materially to a local nonprofit. Many charities allow you to donate or participate in the name of a loved one who has died, so that their legacy continues on through you. The full extent of meaning in your life after loss does not have to come from giving back, but giving can be one way your loved one's death enriches your life and the lives of others.

JUNE 15

" It's not that easy. Loss needs to be experienced. It should be felt in all its beautiful and horrible ways. When your heart is shredded like fraying fabric and dangling in pieces, the scotch tape method isn't going to work long term. Careful stitching and honest grieving is necessary to put things back into place. Maybe not perfectly, but at least in a way so you can breathe again." – CHELSEA TOLMAN

You can try to apply a quick-fix bandage to grief all you want, but at some point, deep surgery and healing must be done to get you to a place of true healing. Allow yourself to go there, either alone or with trusted others, and really feel the experience of grief. It's not easy, but it is enormously worthwhile.

JUNE 16

DID you know that people make playlists for grief? Search "grief playlist," "sad songs," or "music that will make you cry" on Spotify or Pandora to come up with a range of songs perfect for speaking to that ache in your heart. Sometimes listening to grief through someone else's voice and someone else's instrument can help us release and honor the death of our loved one. If you're feeling especially creative, try making your own playlist for grief to have tucked away for hard days.

"It's so curious: one can resist tears and 'behave' very well in the hardest hours of grief. But then someone makes you a friendly sign behind a window, or one notices that a flower that was in bud only yesterday has suddenly blossomed, or a letter slips from a drawer . . . and everything collapses." – COLETTE

Stability is a bit of an illusion in grief. We think we've got our "stuff" together, and then, all of a sudden, a kind glance brings it all crashing down. It's normal to keep trying to build stability in grief. And it's also normal to feel there's no way to be stable. I like to sometimes picture life after loss as my building a tower with blocks and then grief coming to knock it down. It used to make me feel hopeless, but it doesn't anymore. Humans are natural structure builders; losses are natural structure wreckers.

ONE of the best revelations I witnessed in a client was the quiet recognition that she was allowed to leave a party early. A chronic people-pleaser, she was raised to believe that if she attended an event, she had to arrive early and stay until the last guest left for the night. In grief, she found herself exhausted by the thought of parties. She was feeling isolated and cut off from her friends. I gently reminded her that it was more than acceptable to arrive at the party, stay for 10 to 15 minutes, and then make an excuse to go home. If you're putting pressure on yourself to stay for the whole party/meeting/gala/conference, ask yourself, "What's the bare-minimum expectation here?" Reframing social gatherings as 10- to 15-minute appearances is an important tool for protecting your time and energy while still engaging with the people around you.

JUNE 19

" It does not matter how slow you go, as long
as you do not stop." – CONFUCIUS

Progress is progress is progress is progress in grief. Because your grief
is unique to you and only you, you can't measure your healing alongside
somebody else's. The only person you're competing with is the person you
were yesterday. (You can't even compare yourself to the person you were
pre-loss!) So, go, and go slowly, with the wisdom that even the tiniest step
forward is a major win.

JUNE 20

IF you're overwhelmed by the thought of grief or struggling to squeeze grief
into a packed agenda, consider scheduling time to grieve for one hour per
week. Psychologists often suggest that anxious patients schedule time to
worry so that their worrying is kept to a minimum outside that scheduled
"worry time." You might try a similar approach to grief. Having a regular,
designated "grief date" can help you get more accomplished during the week
and allow you to go deep when you're mentally and emotionally prepared
to address grief one-on-one. When you feel grief during the week, make a
note of your emotions in your phone or a private notebook. Then, on your
scheduled "grief date," pull up your notes and work through them one by
one. Giving grief a guaranteed space each week is a surefire way to keep it
from becoming too much to handle. If you're not used to feeling big, hard, or
negative emotions, scheduling time to feel them can help you remember that
these emotions are not life-threatening and that they are part of the normal,
natural human experience.

"I have learned that grief is a vital part of my heart and accept it as a gift that exists alongside joy." – MANDY INGBER

At first, it's hard to believe that grief and joy could ever coexist, but any veteran griever will tell you that the two sit side by side. Contrary to what many people believe, we can experience more than one emotion at a time—and nothing drives that truth home like losing someone we really love. Celebrations are bittersweet, happy days have a crumb of sadness, and beautiful experiences are dark in some way.

JUNE 22

PRACTICE feeling joy. In the immediate aftermath of loss, an emotion as big and positive as joy may seem impossible to feel ever again. And that's perfectly normal—even expected when somebody you love dies. But when the numbness and shock of your loss wear off and you find yourself noticing the world and its beauty again, practice feeling joy. Even if you're angry at flowers for blooming or the sun for shining, tell yourself, "I'm rehearsing joy, so when it comes back, I'll recognize it." Smile, whistle, or add a little bounce to your step if you can. It may take a while to actually experience the full-body emotion of joy, but when you do, you'll recognize it and be ready for it.

JUNE 23

" When one person is missing the whole world
seems empty." — PAT SCHWIEBERT

It seems as if life shouldn't be able to go on without your loved one here, and yet it does. The fact that the whole world doesn't stop immediately when someone dies is one of the hardest and most painful realities of loss. Life goes on ... and you don't want it to. In these moments, take a deep breath and know that the world will seem empty for some time—but not for forever. There is a tiny shred of hope in that.

JUNE 24

AUDACIOUSLY and amazingly, every human in the world will not know that your loved one has died. This is not a wisecrack; I really mean it. When my mom died, I was stunned to learn that there were people in the world who believed she was still alive. They said hello to me in the supermarket and asked how she was as if she were sitting at home, reading in her favorite chair like always. Somehow, they'd missed the memo that she'd passed away. If you find yourself having to be the bearer of bad news, have a script prepared so you're not caught (totally) off guard. Keep it simple. Something like: "I'm sorry to have to tell you this but [insert name] died [insert time here: last spring, a month ago, in October 2011, and so on]." That's all you have to say. Then the ball will be in the other person's court. It may be an uncomfortable conversation, but when you practice it, you won't have to relive your loved one's death every time you break the news. You just have to stick to your script.

"Grief takes many forms, including the absence of grief." – ALISON BECHDEL

If you're a longtime griever, you might know this; if you're a new griever, you might not. There is grief in the absence of grief. Especially in the beginning, it seems like the objective of grieving is to make grief go away, but the longer you grieve and the more you learn about grief, the more you recognize that grief lasts as long as you do. What's wild is when these pockets of non-grief appear—it's almost like you have grief amnesia. For 10 seconds or an hour or three days, you forget that you're grieving. And in that forgetting of grief, there is a whole other kind of grief, because for 10 seconds or an hour or three days, you forgot to be sad that your loved one is no longer there. Having grief amnesia isn't bad; it's just another kind of grieving.

JUNE 26

IT'S okay to take breaks from grief. You might think this isn't possible, and in some ways it's not, but let's see if I can rephrase it this way: it's okay to stop pursuing grief sometimes. Schedule one day a week when you're not going to a support group, Googling your grief symptoms, or processing your grief through journaling, meditation, or another mindfulness tool. Take a day and go easy on the grief work. See how it makes you feel. Of course, this does not mean you can't feel bad or you can't think about your loved one— you most certainly can! Just consider taking 24 hours to turn off the flame under your grief research and put it on the back burner for another day.

JUNE 27

"We do not have to become heroes overnight. Just a step at a time, meeting each thing that comes up, seeing it is not as dreadful as it appeared, discovering we have the strength to stare it down." – ELEANOR ROOSEVELT

Grief is big and scary because it is unknown, and it's really normal to back away from or avoid grief because of all of its unknown-ness. But consider this: grief is a part of you, so is it really entirely unknown? As you explore grief, notice how much of what you're grieving leads back to you: your hopes, dreams, expectations, fears, anxieties, and beliefs. You might know grief better than you think. And that knowing, that wisdom, is a source of strength.

JUNE 28

IF writing or concentrating on reading words is too hard for you in the aftermath of loss (a very normal grief response), consider recording your thoughts instead. Having your experience recorded not only helps you process what you're going through today, but over time, you can see your progress and growth. After you've recorded for a while, go back and listen to your very first recording, your recording from three months ago, and your recording from last week. Having proof of your progress is another way to build up your strength and confidence after a loved one dies. Not sure where to start? Use the Voice Memos app on an Apple device or google "audio journal app" for an Android or Google device. A traditional tape recorder is also a wonderful option if you have access to one.

"In the Old Testament, a person in grief tore his robe . . .
There was weeping and wailing. But in our nutty society,
the person who 'keeps it together,' who's 'so brave,' and
who 'looks so great – you'd never know,' that's who is
applauded. Grief is not the opposite of faith. Mourning
is not the opposite of hope." – JENNIFER SAAKE

In the Western world, it's considered inappropriate and even immature to express grief in highly visible ways. This is unfortunate, because the process of grieving is not exactly a silent or put-together one. Know that while the whole world is not necessarily a safe place for grief, there are spaces and places, perhaps even in your own home, where you can wail, keen, thrash, and tear your clothes if you want to.

JUNE 30

I grieved my mom in the front seat of my dad's pickup truck. It was parked in the garage, and I snuck out there almost every night leading up to her death to scream, cry, beat the headrest, and plead with the powers that be to let her live. What I didn't realize at the time was that I was practicing an ancient ritual: keening (wailing, crying out, vocally lamenting) for the death of a loved one. I encourage you to try keening in a place that feels safe for you. When tears are flowing, try moving air from the back of your throat out through your mouth as if you're getting ready to moan or sing. Then let the noises flow and allow grief to pull them out of your mouth. This heartbreaking expression of grief can help you feel heard, that your grief is being fully expressed. It's natural and normal to want to howl our pain to the sky.

JULY 1

" You can be happy again, but you can never be happy and the same again." – SALLIE TISDALE

"How to be happy again" may not be the first thing you Google after a loved one dies, but regaining happiness, joy, and even laughter is on the minds of most grievers. As crappy as we feel right now, we want to know that it's not going to be this way forever—and beyond that, that grief hasn't broken our ability to feel cheerful and upbeat. You are not alone in wondering whether happiness will return; I assure you it will . . . just maybe not in the same way you knew it before.

JULY 2

IF you're sick of feeling down in the dumps, check out a comedian's take on grief through stand-up. Comics Kelli Dunham, Patton Oswalt, Laurie Kilmartin, and Tig Notaro all joke about grief and loss in their routines. Whether they are laughing about their own diagnoses and hardships or speaking about the deaths of people they really, really loved, it's refreshing to see a humorous take on grief. (P.S. If you're sensitive when it comes to gallows humor, bypass grief jokes and stand-up routines until you're ready to hear them.)

" No one saves us but ourselves. No one can and no one
may. We ourselves must walk the path." – BUDDHA

As much as group grief support, therapy, and other forms of grief guidance are helpful in the aftermath of loss, in the end, we must do the work
of healing ourselves. All the aid in the world is of no use to us if we don't
examine it and then apply it in our own lives. At the end of the day, no one is
going to save you in grief; you must save yourself. The good news is, all that's
required is a desire to try, to walk the path that's been laid before you.

JULY 4

IT'S normal to lean on the wisdom or attitude of your loved one in your
healing. Many grievers attribute their openheartedness, their positive
outlook, or their fortitude to a loved one who has died. Try this: Get out
a piece of paper and close your eyes. Envision your loved one sitting or
standing before you and write down any descriptive words that come to
mind. What traits did your loved one have in life that are helping you now
in their death? What have they taught you that you're using or leaning on
for help now? If they could give you any reassurance or piece of advice,
what would it be? If you cannot "hear" your loved one, try to sense them in
your body. If you cannot sense them in your body, imagine what they would
say to you if they could.

JULY 5

" Grieving is like embarking upon a journey toward an unknown destination, against your will: it is incredibly difficult, heartbreaking, and time consuming – and there aren't any shortcuts." – JOANNE FINK

If someone is selling you a quick fix for grief, run away—far away! Grief, by nature, is long term, complex, and absolutely unique to you. What works for one person will not necessarily work for you, and vice versa. You've got to be able to follow your own map, learn to read your own compass, and find your own way. That's not to say the tools and advice of others aren't helpful; there are just no simple ways to bypass grieving.

JULY 6

SOMETIMES it's helpful to think of grief as a really long road trip, and it can be refreshing to play road trip–style games while grieving. Try the "ABC game," where you name 26 different things your loved one liked, starting with the letter *A* and ending with *Z*. If letters like *Q*, *X*, and *Z* are tricky, use your loved one's first initial instead. Or play "I Spy," where you spot grief in interesting places, like in your favorite TV show or a book you're reading: "I spy with my little eye . . . someone grieving!" These games can help normalize the fact that grief, in some form or fashion, is everywhere.

" We can't 'move on' or forgive at the click of someone's fingers." – SOPHIE HANNAH

Forgiveness is practically built into the experience of grieving, but despite the strong emotions and opinions of others, we can forgive only on *our* time line. We can't be rushed into forgiveness for the sake of making someone else (or our dead loved one!) feel better; we can forgive only when it feels true and right to us. Take heart in knowing that it's extremely rare to forgive overnight and that many grieving people are in the same boat you are.

IF you're struggling to forgive yourself, your loved one, or someone else, but you aren't quite ready, consider saying something like "I'm trying to forgive [insert name]" or "I intend to forgive [insert name]." This lets both you and the people around you know that you're working on forgiveness, but you're not 100 percent there yet. It's a simple way to set an intention and announce it without pledging inauthentic full-fledged forgiveness before you're ready.

JULY 9

"At the end of the day, we can endure much more than we think we can. Nothing is absolute. Everything changes, everything moves, everything revolves, everything flies and goes away." – FRIDA KAHLO

When I work with a client, there comes a point, without fail, when they look back on their progress and say something like "Wow. I can't believe I survived that. I can't believe I did that right after my loved one died. I can't believe I'm still standing." Disbelief and wonder can come with life after loss, as if we don't recognize that our own legs are what got us here. Take a moment today to marvel at your strength. You are the person, the force, who got you to this place.

JULY 10

WRITE a letter to the person you were on the day your loved one died. Describe the circumstances of where you are now, gently and compassionately comparing them to the circumstances of your life then. Thank yourself for having faith in yourself to move ahead, even if motion seemed impossible. Acknowledge your past self's understandable fear and pain on that day. Let yourself know that you're taking care of the both of you and that, together, you'll continue walking the path of grief. Return to this exercise anytime you need a boost of faith in your own strength and your ability to keep moving forward. If you're struggling with this exercise, ask a friend or family member to provide perspective on where you were then versus where you are today. You might be surprised by your progress.

" We must walk consciously only part way toward our goal, and then leap in the dark to our success." – HENRY DAVID THOREAU

Half of healing comprises the tangible tools, systems, practices, and mindsets that provide you with structure, foundation, and security. The other half of healing is keeping the faith that healing will happen at all. One is very visible; the other is invisible. We need both to live well after loss.

JULY 12

YOU can make life after loss a lot simpler by narrowing down your list of "have-tos." Have-tos are tasks you must do daily in order to survive. These are required chores and essentials such as letting the dog in and out, going to work and returning home, and feeding yourself (and others in your household). Your list of have-tos should not include luxury or onetime tasks like getting a haircut, taking the car to the carwash, or going out for drinks. In addition, when someone (a person or institution) presents you with a task that is not on your have-to list, consider it a request to withdraw energy from your grief energy account. Would you like to make this transaction? The choice is up to you.

JULY 13

"In three words I can sum up everything I've learned about life: it goes on." – ROBERT FROST

While it seems like it should, life does not stop the day our loved one dies. I used to resent that fact, until I framed it in a new way: if death were powerful enough to *literally pause life*, I don't know that I would choose to un-pause it. I would be stuck forever on the day my mom died, and I would've missed out on the past seven years of living. While I would still trade those seven years to have my mom back, I can't say I'd want death to have the final say on whether I got to keep on living. Being forced to rejoin the living helped propel me forward at a time when I needed it most.

JULY 14

CREATE a small daily ritual that honors your loved one. The ritual should take less than 60 seconds and be able to be performed anywhere, so that you can continue to do it while traveling. It could be something like greeting your bedroom ceiling each morning with "Good morning, [insert name of your loved one]," listening to a cheerful voice mail your loved one left on your phone, or pinning a brooch or medal of theirs to your collar. This small, meaningful ritual can help ease your fears that your loved one's memory will somehow be left in the past. It's impossible to forget about someone when their memory is hardwired into your daily routine.

" You will survive and you will find purpose in the chaos.
Moving on doesn't mean letting go." – MARY VANHAUTE

Continuing to live does not mean consenting to forget. You are not a bucket with a limited capacity. No, you are an ever-changing container with the amazing ability to accommodate not only your life and your love, but the life and love of the person who died. It is possible to hold many, many lost loved ones in one body and still keep trudging forward. Progress does not mean leaving your loved ones behind. It means taking them with you and keeping them alongside you for the remainder of your ride.

JULY 16

WHILE your body has finite bounds, your heart does not. Practice feeling your heart expand and grow as you make room for your loved one to live inside it. Close your eyes and imagine them building a permanent home in your heart. What color is the house? How is it furnished? Does it have a garden, a game room, or a whirlpool tub? Where in this house is your loved one most often: on a recliner, in the kitchen, or on the front porch? Picturing where your loved one lives in your heart can help you feel like they are more rooted in the present, instead of an abstract vision that is left in the past. Carry them forward with you, in a custom home in your heart.

JULY 17

"I wanted a perfect ending. Now I've learned, the hard way, that some poems don't rhyme, and some stories don't have a clear beginning, middle, and end. Life is about not knowing, having to change, taking the moment and making the best of it, without knowing what's going to happen next." – GILDA RADNER

Uncertainty is a hallmark of loss. Grief, and all its unexpected twists and turns, does a great job of upending any expectation we have that life is predictable or perfect. While it's upsetting and disheartening to realize that life is not always clean and tidy, it's also hopeful in a twisted sort of way. If life isn't perfect, you don't have to try to make it that way. You simply have to try your best with the circumstances you're given, because nobody knows what's going to happen next.

JULY 18

MAKE your home a safe place for grief. Using a large piece of construction paper or a legal pad, create a list of "House Rules for Grief." These can be as simple as "We are allowed to cry about anything without explanation" and "No judging or advice giving allowed!" You can also make your house rules as silly or as personal as "Whoever uses the last tissue has to buy more!" or "No one sits at Daddy's place at the table." When you're done making your list of house rules, tack it to the refrigerator or a bulletin board for all to see.

" Hope is the feeling we have that the feeling we have
is not permanent." – MIGNON MCLAUGHLIN

Some people see hope as this pie-in-the-sky portrait of where they'll be one day, a land without aches, pains, troubles, or fears. In grief, the picture of hope is scaled down, a statement that says simply, "It won't always be this way." Believing that something different is coming is often the only thing that makes the present moment bearable. We find we can live in pain just a little bit longer if we know a respite from that pain is inevitably on its way.

JULY 20

MAKE a list of things you'd like to do. These can be grand, lifetime schemes similar to those on a bucket list ("ride in a hot-air balloon," "meet a favorite celebrity," "see the Nile") or small, everyday pleasures you're excited to return to down the road ("read a book from start to finish," "drive past the funeral home without holding my breath," "sleep through the night"). Then, once a month, check your list. You may find you've made progress on it without even realizing it—it took me a couple of weeks to recognize that I was sleeping through the night again—or, if you haven't, mindfully plan ways to achieve your goals. There's no limit to the number of items allowed on your list. Think of it merely as a loose outline of your desires for your life after loss.

JULY 21

"Especially with grief and heartbreak, you can go through these things and think, 'I will never be whole again.'" – ADAM SILVERA

It's normal to view loss as a destructive force that damages or even breaks us beyond all repair. And in some ways, yes, you cannot be whole in the way you once were. But what I and so many other grievers have discovered is a new definition for wholeness, wholeness that includes the big-time experience of loss. Instead of viewing *yourself* as broken, why not view *your old definition of wholeness* as broken? For example, instead of telling yourself, "I am broken," try telling yourself, "My old view of 'wholeness' is broken. I am learning to see the brokenness brought about by loss as a part of my new definition of 'wholeness.'" Your wholeness does not exclude your brokenness. In fact, your brokenness is an integral part of the whole picture of you.

JULY 22

SOMETHING that contributes greatly to a sense of wholeness is the feeling of being totally present in the moment. Try doing something you always do, but doing it *really slowly*, so you notice every single aspect of it. I enjoy making a cup of tea very slowly: filling up the teapot with water, standing by as it cranks to a rolling boil, tearing open a tea bag, tying the tea bag to the handle of my favorite mug, pouring the water over the bag, and watching the steam rise from the cup. At first, making tea slowly felt excruciating. But with continued practice, it's become an activity that helps me focus, breathe, and come back to the richness of the present moment. Next time you're feeling less than whole, consider brushing your hair, filing paperwork, folding laundry, or watering your houseplants *very slowly*.

" Grief resets the clock of life to before and after." – LYNDA CHELDELIN FELL

Loss splits us, and the time line of our lives, in two. When we experience the death of someone we love, there is a distinct moment when we stop marking time with minutes, hours, and days and start marking it with simply "before" and "after." It's normal to feel as if you're operating on a totally different schedule from the rest of the world . . . because you are.

JULY 24

BEING obsessed with or preoccupied by time or dates is a common side effect of grief. My mom died on December 26, and on the 26th day of every month, for months after my mom died, I struggled to get out of bed, stay focused, and speak to other people. It was as if, each month, my body were pulling me right back to that date. If you're experiencing these full-body flashbacks, and you have the financial and practical means to do so, take these "griefiversary" dates as full or half days off from work and other obligations for at least the first six months after your loss. Honoring the fact that you may be more consumed by your grief than usual on that day is a loving way to let yourself remember the person you've lost. You can always decide to go into work or perform your regular routines after all, but giving yourself the space and permission to do nothing is powerfully self-compassionate.

JULY 25

" The great soul is the person who has taken
on the task of change." – GARY ZUKAV

Grief requires us to change our lives at an external level, but also at an internal one. If you find yourself questioning your faith; your trust in the world, yourself, or others; or your belief that "everything happens for a reason," know that you are not alone. This is common among grievers. The death of a loved one doesn't just shake up our outside world; it messes with our inside world, too, and there is surreal solidarity in knowing you are not the only one facing change on so many fronts.

JULY 26

SOCIETY has plenty of rituals and expectations for mourning someone we love who has died, but what about mourning things we can't see, hear, or touch, like hopes, dreams, belief systems, and personality traits? Try this: Pick up a few flat stones outside or purchase a bag of river rocks from a craft store. With a permanent marker or paint pen, write your name on one of the rocks, to represent your old self, and on the others, write all the intangible things you're grieving. These can be things like "faith," "trust in myself," "creativity," "the belief that the good guys always win," and so on. When you're done, bury your "old self" along with your "losses," saying something like "I acknowledge that in losing my loved one, I also lost my old self and [insert invisible losses]." If you don't have access to a place to bury your stones, consider safely tossing them into a lake or pond.

"Grief lasts longer than sympathy, which is one of the tragedies of the grieving." – ELIZABETH MCCRACKEN

At some point, the flowers stop coming, the freezer is emptied of all of the casseroles, and the mailbox is no longer packed with sympathy cards. It appears as if the sympathy and well-wishes of family, friends, and coworkers has run dry. In most cases, it's not a lack of caring on the part of the people around you; it's the reality that everyone has a life to live outside the loss of your loved one. Your life now *is* the loss of your loved one, so for you, the grief goes on. At this time, it's more important than ever to connect with others who are also grieving.

IT'S normal for friendships to become strained in the aftermath of loss. And it's also normal for you to be too exhausted, too overwhelmed, and too heartbroken to have the energy to reach out to your friends right away. While losing a friendship is painful, it's okay to let it slide for the moment while you tend to yourself and your grief. When you're feeling ready, connect to your friend through a letter or email message. Say something like "I know it's been a while since we've spoken, but I wanted to let you know that I was really hurt when you [stopped calling me on Sundays]. You may have a good reason for it, but the story I'm telling myself is [you thought I was too "negative"]. I would really hate if this story were true and am open to hearing your thoughts on this. I miss having you as a friend in my life. I hope to hear from you soon." If they respond thoughtfully, consider resuming the friendship. If they meet you with defensiveness, anger, or silence, consider the friendship lost and seek out people who are more accepting of you and your grief.

JULY 29

"Although it's natural to forget your power after you lose a loved one, the truth is that after a breakup, divorce, or death, there remains an ability within you to create a new reality." — LOUISE HAY AND DAVID KESSLER

While the death of a loved one can make you feel powerless, it cannot take away your power. Whether you realize it or not, you have a choice in every moment to make the next moment better or worse than the one you're living now. This is not always an *easy* choice, but it is there all the same. What will you feel, think, be, or do next?

JULY 30

TASK your friends with helping you break out of your routine. Enlist 5 to 10 friends as "activity directors" and encourage them to invite you to tag along with whatever they're doing: brunch, the movies, a workout class, hiking, a neighborhood softball game, and so on. Let them know that even if you decline some or most of the time, what matters most is that they don't stop inviting you to do things with them. Each new invitation you receive is an opportunity to connect with your friend, try a new experience, or prove to yourself that you are capable of making the choice to do something different or novel at any time.

" Grief can destroy you – or focus you. You can decide a relationship was all for nothing if it had to end in death, and you alone. Or you can realize that every moment of it had more meaning than you dared to recognize . . . you're driven to your knees not by the weight of the loss but by gratitude for what preceded the loss." – DEAN KOONTZ

Western society often portrays death as failure. In other words, "If something we love is going to die, it's a waste of time to love it in the first place. What's the point if it's going to end in death?" Only you can decide if you agree or disagree with this mindset. For me, death does not negate all the love and warmth and memories that came before it. While my mother's death was and continues to be the worst thing that has ever happened to me, I refuse to throw the baby out with the bathwater. I wouldn't trade the 21 years I spent with her for anything.

AUGUST 1

GRATITUDE is a struggle for many grievers. It's understandable, because someone's saying, "Just be grateful!" makes you want to punch that person in the face. Try reframing gratitude not as something you're thankful for but as something that is keeping you alive in the aftermath of loss. Don't make a list of things you're grateful for; make a list of things that are giving you life—like seeing your dog's face or knowing there's a box of strawberry popsicles in the freezer. Instead of asking, "What am I grateful for?" ask, "What in my life is giving me life?" This will move the grand, overly joyful gesture of gratitude into a place that's more accessible in grief.

AUGUST 2

" Most people don't ever feel okay or all right about the loss of a loved one. [Acceptance] is about accepting the reality that our loved one is physically gone and recognizing that this new reality is the permanent reality. We will never like this reality or make it okay, but eventually we accept it. We learn to live with it. It is the new norm with which we must learn to love. This is where our final healing and adjustment can take a firm hold, despite the fact that healing often looks and feels like an unattainable state." – ELISABETH KÜBLER-ROSS

In experiencing the death of a loved one, you received one of the worst hands life can deal us. You don't ever have to like it, but you do have to learn to live with it. Getting to a place of acceptance with your loss is not about your feelings about it (for example, this *sucks*); it's about acknowledging that what happened . . . happened, and that it is possible for you to heal inclusive of your loss. If you expect healing to look like getting back to the life you had before, you will never attain it; if you reframe healing as doing the best you can under the circumstances, you will get closer and closer to it every day.

AUGUST 3

REACH out and connect with one of your favorite grief experts, authors, speakers, Instagram therapists, celebrities, or mental health role models. Most people working in the grief space are open to chatting, or are at least available to respond to an email. Share something you love about their work, like a tip that's helped you, or send a photo of your loved one. You might just find yourself making friends with a real-life grief "influencer!"

"Grief is so human, and it hits everyone at one point or another, at least, in their lives. If you love, you will grieve, and that's just given." – KAY REDFIELD JAMISON

Love and grief are inexplicably and permanently intertwined. When we share our heart and soul with someone, it makes sense that we are devastated by their death. Grief is a reflection of our deep, meaningful, and important connection to our loved one. It hurts to lose them, and that's normal and natural to feel.

AUGUST 5

THERE'S nothing like a good TV binge, and fortunately for grievers, the streaming industry is getting more and more comfortable addressing grief up close and personal. Series like *This Is Us* (Hulu with HBO Max), *Dead to Me* (Netflix), and *Sorry for Your Loss* (Facebook Watch) all do a tremendous job of covering loss and its aftermath. In each series, you can find examples of grief through the lenses of family dynamics, taboo circumstances, uncovering secrets after a loss, and more. If you're looking to connect with grief from the comfort of your couch, google "TV shows about grief" and see what's available right now on your streaming platforms. Consider making your binge session a group activity and invite friends, family, or fellow grievers to watch along with you. You might just open up the door to new conversations about what it's like to grieve.

AUGUST 6

"Grief is an extremely emotional experience. It also does a number on your brain." — BARBARA FANE

"Grief brain" is a very real side effect of grief. Forgetfulness, racing thoughts, and feeling foggy or numb are commonly reported experiences after the loss of a loved one. If you feel your brain is at maximum capacity or has gone AWOL, you are not alone. Be gentle with yourself and know that you're not crazy; you're just grieving.

AUGUST 7

BUY yourself a stack of sticky notes and write reminders for yourself all over your home. These can be practical ("Your car keys are in the foyer," "Make an appointment for Friday at 3:00," "You don't have carpool duty this week!") or motivational ("Take it one day at a time," "It's not your job to solve grief; just to experience it," "You've got this"). It may seem silly at first to litter your living space with bright notes for your brain, but these reminders can prove to be an enormous help when your keys or your faith in yourself go missing for a little bit.

" Where you used to be, there is a hole in the world, which I find myself constantly walking around in the daytime, and falling in at night." – EDNA ST. VINCENT MILLAY

After a full day of being "on," it's normal to feel like your grief emerges in full force at night. It's easy to avoid grief during the day—when work, family, errands, friends, chores, and appearing fine take top priority. Busyness is a familiar and often welcome distraction from the pain of grief. But grief doesn't go away because you're doing something else. It patiently waits for you to have nothing left to do, and then it makes its appearance. Allow yourself to spend time with it when it shows up. Grief is not out to ruin your day or make you miserable; it just wants to be heard amid the noise of your everyday life.

MANY grievers place themselves into one of two camps, "doing well" or "grieving," as if grieving were the opposite of doing well. In reality, grief is a sign of your health, wholeheartedness, and humanness. I, and others, would be concerned if you *didn't* mourn the death of your loved one. What if, instead of classifying grief as "not doing well," you thought of it as evidence that you're right where you need to be? Try replacing judgmental statements like "It's not okay to grieve," "I should be over it by now," and "There must be something wrong with me" with more neutral statements like "This is what naturally happens when someone you love dies," "My grief is a response to having my heart broken," and "It's okay to grieve about this; it's something worth grieving about."

AUGUST 10

"We want to put things in boxes and wrap it up with a nice bow, but unfortunately with losing people, there is no box, and there is no bow." – JONATHAN VAN NESS

Unlike other big life milestones (graduation, marriage, buying a house), there is no set order of events for grief. It's a totally out-of-order, out-of-the-box experience that we learn to navigate in our own ways. We're not handed a rule book for "how to grieve"; we simply know that we must.

AUGUST 11

YOU can try to compartmentalize grief all you want, but it has a sneaky, irritating way of infiltrating every aspect of our lives. Try picturing grief as a never-ending game of Whac-A-Mole, with grief and its chittering laugh popping up in places and relationships where you least expect it (hello, grief on a grocery trip/first date/job interview). Each time grief appears, I invite you to shout something silly like "Oh, not *you* again!" And then, if you can muster a laugh, *laugh*! Laughter helps us break up hard or painful emotions and move them out of the body. And to me, there's nothing quite like laughing at grief when it has tracked you down *yet again*.

" When we think about healing, we tend to only think about the gentle parts. Rest and recovery. Massages and a lot of naps. Juice and healthy, nourishing meals. But sometimes healing is hard. Sometimes it hurts as much as, if not more than, the thing that broke us in the first place. Sometimes healing is about breaking what didn't break all the way through, so that we can put things back together the way they're supposed to be. So we can finally mend." – STEPHENIE ZAMORA

Do you ever feel like there's more grief under your grief? Like you've peeled back the wallpaper covering your grief only to find out that you have to take the whole wall down because it's not structurally sound? Healing from grief is a lot of hard work. It's a figurative demolition of your old life and a rebuilding of a new one. And sometimes the walls that didn't get taken down with the death of your loved one need to be torn down in the aftermath. It's not because there's anything wrong with the walls; it's because those walls are no longer a fit in life after loss.

GRIEF affects all areas of our lives, and our finances are no exception. Whether you find yourself shelling out money for a loved one's funeral services or receiving a posthumous windfall, your bank account has probably been affected by grief. Schedule a date to assess how grief has impacted your finances. It may be uncomfortable to look at the reality of your finances after a loved one dies, but money is one area of your life where it's better to be certain than remain in the dark. Call on a trusted financial adviser or seek support from your local bank if you're unsure where to start.

AUGUST 14

" The way I will truly honor my mother's memory is not with a big act, but through my daily choices: to be compassionate with myself . . . to give myself freely to those I love . . . and to live fully and completely while I have the chance." – CAMILLE PAGÁN

Recovery from the death of a loved one rarely looks like grand gestures and soaring moments of triumph. In fact, living well after loss more often looks like gradually giving ourselves and the people around us just a little more compassion, just a little more permission, and just a little more love every single day. Healing doesn't need to be grand to be worthwhile; it's the littlest moments that make the biggest difference.

AUGUST 15

SOME grievers feel an enormous pressure to hold back tears or what they consider "negative" emotions because their loved one wouldn't want them to be sad. Of course our loved ones would not want to see us in pain, but consider this: we do not grieve to satisfy our loved ones; we grieve to soothe and heal ourselves. If you feel you can't grieve because your loved one would be disappointed, write them a letter asking them to release you from the expectation of positivity. For example, "Dear [insert loved one's name], I know that it would hurt you to see me crying and mourning your death, but I need you to understand that I love you so much that your death impacts me at a very emotional level. I believe that I will be okay one day, but today, I need to express *all* my feelings."

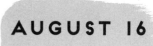

"But in all of the sadness . . . You've got to remember that grief isn't the absence of love. Grief is the proof that love is still there." – TESSA SHAFFER

We don't grieve things that don't matter to us. Grieving is just another way of saying, "I care a whole, whole lot about the person I've lost, and it's hard not having them here." The next time you start to beat yourself up for feeling grief, gently remind yourself that grief is not a sign that something is wrong with you; it's evidence that you had a strong connection to the person you've lost.

AUGUST 17

RECONNECT with someone who served as a role model in your life. This could be a career mentor, a high school coach, a college professor, or a religious leader. Anyone you felt a special bond with who guided you or taught you in some way is fair game. Reach out and invite them to a phone call, video conversation, or, if possible, a face-to-face meeting with you. Share your loss story with them and see what wisdom or advice they impart to you. Your role model may have special knowledge about your strengths and your talents that other friends and family may not. Plus, they probably have a grief story of their own to share.

AUGUST 18

"Life doesn't get easier or more forgiving. We get stronger and more resilient." — STEVE MARABOLI

There's a myth floating around that "time heals all wounds," as if allowing enough time to pass makes the loss of our loved one easier to handle or less painful to remember. In reality, life after the loss of a loved one doesn't get easier or less painful. Instead, we learn how to *manage* our heartache and face grief as it comes. The illusion is that we've finally reached a life with less grief. The truth is that the same amount of grief is present; we've just become better at adapting to it.

AUGUST 19

IDENTIFY a handful of "access points" for your grief: movies, music, scents, YouTube videos, and so on. These should be emotionally triggering stimuli that prompt you to grieve. Whenever you're feeling stuck or that you haven't allowed yourself to express your grief in a while, tap into these sources to unlock unexpressed grief. My go-to is the 1944 film *National Velvet*. At the end of the movie, Velvet's mother tells her that "there is a time for everything, even a time to die." Hearing this soft wisdom handed down from mother to daughter opens the floodgates for me and, no matter how long it's been since I've grieved, allows me to access my emotions again and again.

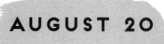

AUGUST 20

❝I do not believe that sheer suffering teaches. If suffering alone taught, all the world would be wise, since everyone suffers. To suffering must be added mourning, understanding, patience, love, openness, and the willingness to remain vulnerable.❞ — ANNE MORROW LINDBERGH

In and of itself, suffering is not a pathway to self-improvement. Anyone who thinks experiencing the death of a loved one automatically makes you stronger, better, or more enlightened is very sadly mistaken. In order to help us in any way, suffering must be combined with something else: meaning, purpose, perspective, love. Suffering does not equal enlightenment. It's what we add to our suffering that counts.

AUGUST 21

IN the aftermath of loss, it's normal to be overwhelmed and seek a sympathetic ear. But sometimes we worry we might be an emotional burden to our friends and family. To alleviate this concern, develop a mini-script for requesting permission before you rant to someone. Before launching into your awful-day story, tell your friend/family member, "I had a really hard day and would be so grateful for a space to brain-dump. Is now a good time to text/call/chat? If not, no pressure. I can talk to you tomorrow at work/ next week over coffee/via email." Allowing your friend or family member an opportunity to opt out can help them feel they're not taking on all your grief out of the blue and will reassure you that when they *do* make themselves available, they genuinely have the time and space to listen.

AUGUST 22

" I've found that there is always some beauty
left – in nature, sunshine, freedom, in yourself;
these can all help you." – ANNE FRANK

Sometimes it's difficult to see beauty in life after loss, but take a look
around. Of the 100 percent that is your life, is 1 percent beautiful? If not,
how about .01 percent or .001 percent? Any speck of beauty you see helps
beauty find its way back to you after the death of a loved one. Start by visualizing the smile or spirit of your loved one. That's a source of beauty.

AUGUST 23

CLOSE your eyes, take a deep breath, and reopen them. What around you
is beautiful? Is it a plant on your desk, a cloud outside, or a photograph on
your dresser? Even in the darkness of grief, you are surrounded by beauty. If
you're struggling to find anything beautiful, first practice noticing. Simply
observe that an object exists. When you're ready, start describing ways that
the object is beautiful: "I really like how its petals catch the light," "That
cloud is shaped like my favorite animal," "Her smile in this picture always
makes me laugh." Then, when you're ready, mentally or verbally classify the
object as beautiful: "Wow! That's beautiful." If this is still too hard, try saying, "I'll bet that's beautiful" or "I know I'll find that beautiful one day."

" Bereavement is the deepest initiation into the mysteries of human life, an initiation more searching and profound than even happy love." – DEAN INGE

To grieve is to join the ranks of "those who have gone before." Everyone who has ever lived has grieved in some way, and will be grieved themselves. Grief takes us into the stratosphere of searching, and in searching for answers about the loss of our loved one, we understand that the human race has been searching and searching and searching for a very long time. It's normal to wonder about the meaning of loss and question why death exists. As you look for answers about the loss of your loved one, know that you are not alone. Your experience is shared by many.

AUGUST 25

EVERY now and then, I'll hear a story about a grieving person who visited a medium looking for answers about their loved one. My beliefs on mediums fall on both sides—I've been scammed, and I've been pleasantly surprised—so I won't tell you what to do with your time or your money. What I will tell you is that if you're considering a visit to your local psychic, intuitive, or reader, do your research. Get recommendations from friends and family, search online listings like Yelp or Google Reviews, and see if there's a mini-session or group event you can attend before dropping the megabucks for a one-on-one session. Attend your session with an open mind, and be open to what the medium says. If you become uncomfortable, know that you, as a client and paying customer, have permission to leave the session at any time. Take notes if you can, or record the session. You might want to revisit it later.

AUGUST 26

"Grief jumps out at you when you're least expecting it." – DOMINIC COOPER

Every griever knows that grief pops out at the most unexpected moments. (I once fled a department store because a woman ahead of me in the checkout line looked just like my mom.) There's no way to predict when grief will arrive. If you're feeling caught off guard by grief, you are not alone. It catches every grieving person by surprise.

AUGUST 27

IF you shared a home with the person who died, you know the unique agony of continuing to receive magazine subscriptions and junk mail addressed to your loved one. These magazines and little pieces of paper can be enormous triggers for grief and can send you spiraling when you least expect it. For one month, place every piece of junk mail you receive for your loved one into a pile. Then, at the end of that month, make a list of all the senders' names and phone numbers. (If a phone number isn't listed on the piece of mail itself, you can usually find contact information by doing a quick Google search.) When you've got all the phone numbers ready, work your way down the list, calling each sender to request that your loved one be unsubscribed from their mailing list. If letting perfect strangers know that your loved one has died is too much for you, outsource this task to a friend or family member. It's an easy-enough job for anyone who tells you, "Let me know if there's anything I can do."

AUGUST 28

" Loss doesn't have an expiration date."
— EMILY MCDOWELL AND DR. KELSEY CROWE

Grief has an infinite shelf life. It will never run out or go bad. It exists alongside us for the rest of our lives. The good news is, there's no better or worse time to start processing your grief. Because it never expires, you can delve into grief at any time. The less-than-good news is that you must find space for grief in your figurative pantry in every single season of your life. It's like that big old bag of rice that gets lugged from home to home every time you move. It's not exciting, and certainly not trendy or fun, but it's a staple and a necessity all the same.

AUGUST 29

ONE of the most painful experiences my clients report is that no one around them says their loved one's name after their death. It's as if the world is willingly forgetting, and there's a very real fear that their loved one will be erased from their life. In these instances, I remind my clients that they need to prompt friends and family to say their loved one's name. If you wish the people around you would speak your loved one's name, ask them a question like "Look at this picture I found of [loved one's name]. Can you share the story of what happened that day?" Asking for a story instead of demanding your loved one's name be spoken is a gentler way of inviting their name into the mouths of others. Additionally, speaking their name gives others permission to do the same; they'll understand it's something you want, not something that makes you uncomfortable.

AUGUST 30

" Perhaps grief is not about empty, but full. The full breath of life that includes death. The completeness, the cycles, the depth, the richness, the process, the continuity and the treasure of the moment that is gone the second you are aware of it." — ALYSIA REINER

There's an illusion that grief is a nothingness, a void or an abyss in which everything awful and dark and heartbreaking lives. The longer I sit with my grief, the more I understand that grief is a richness, one of life's "expert levels" that we unlock when someone we really love dies. Recognizing that death is a part of life adds weight and dimension to the everyday—a beautiful and sad knowing that nothing lasts forever. A life with grief is not a curse; it's a reminder to treasure the things we love about our lives . . . because one day we will be gone, too.

AUGUST 31

CONSIDER asking another griever to be your pen pal. There's something special and sacred about writing and receiving a handwritten letter, and sharing your thoughts on life after loss with another human who is also sharing their thoughts on life after loss can be profoundly healing. Find a pen pal to connect with by searching "grief pen pal" on Google or by reaching out to someone whose grief story resonates with you in an online or in-person grief support group. See if you can stretch the boundaries and connect with a grieving person of a different race, gender, religion, generation, or nationality. If you feel inclined, deck out your mailings with stickers, doodles, or a photo of your loved one.

" What they never tell you about grief is that missing someone is the simple part." — GAIL CALDWELL

A huge chunk of grief is longing, physically and emotionally *aching*, for our lost loved one. But grief is so much more than that. It's about everything that led up to their death (their life and our memories with them) and everything that comes after (the life we are forced to live without them). Missing someone is at the root of grief, but it is not the entirety of it. Grief has many, many layers, and we, as grievers, are tasked with slowly peeling them away.

ONE of the most difficult parts of grief is having to go through a loved one's belongings and decide what to keep and what to get rid of. Death has a tendency to compound our attachment to our loved one's possessions. It's tempting to keep everything because your loved one will never touch, wear, or own anything new. It's also tempting to burn everything so you don't have to face the pain of deciding what happens to it. When you start to tackle this difficult task, try this: Set a timer for 10 minutes. After 10 minutes of reminiscing and decision making, check in with yourself. Would you like to continue? Would you like to be done for the day? It's up to you. If you decide to continue, set the timer for another 10 minutes and keep checking in with yourself emotionally throughout the process. If you decide not to continue, thank yourself for accomplishing as much as you could in this moment and try again at another time. It's more than okay for this part of grief to take a long time.

SEPTEMBER 3

"Grief is a very complicated monster. There's no real exorcising of it. It has a different form every day." – YANCE FORD

One of my clients referred to grief as a shapeshifter, and I can't think of a better way to describe it. Every single day, grief becomes something else, as if every 24 hours reveals a new grief feature we haven't seen before. People who haven't grieved think grief is all about dealing with big emotions, and that's partially true. But it is also about learning to roll with the punches—the unexpected, shapeshifting nature of life after loss.

SEPTEMBER 4

WHILE it's easier and more convenient to mail a check or make a donation online, consider showing up for a charity event in person. This could be a 5K walk, a silent auction, or a fundraising dinner. Most people start or join charities because they are personally invested in the cause they are championing. So, the odds of connecting with someone with a grief story are pretty good. Introducing yourself as a newcomer and asking, "What brought you to this charity specifically?" is a great way to break the ice. If you're looking for an event to attend, ask around to see what charities family and friends embrace. Or do a Google search for local charities that support a cause close to your heart.

"She was no longer wrestling with the grief, but could sit down with it as a lasting companion and make it a sharer in her thoughts." – GEORGE ELIOT

This is one of my favorite quotes about grief, because it paints a picture of grief as a "lasting companion." There's something gentle and reassuring about seeing grief as a collaborative partner. (It's a drastic turnaround from society's perception of grief as an enemy to be vanquished.) When we stop fighting grief or insisting that it go away, we can welcome it in as a companion and collaborate with it to support us as we move forward.

WRITE a letter to yourself from your future self, honoring the journey on which grief has accompanied you. Picture yourself 6 months, 1 year, 5 years, or 10 years, into the future, looking back at who you are now. What would you most like to say to the person you are now? What are you proud of? What feels enormous and insurmountable now that your future self sees differently? How has your grief changed shape and size and expression? What have you accomplished in the aftermath of your loss that you would like to thank yourself for? These letters can go in as many directions as you like. One recurring theme I see with my clients that may be helpful for you is this: our future selves know that where we are *right now* is not where we are stuck forever. And having hope that this will pass, even from an imagined "future self," is incredibly powerful.

SEPTEMBER 7

"The fall is not the hard part . . . rock bottom is not the hard part . . . I couldn't believe it. I realized with overwhelming certainty that . . . the hard part was the return, because the return required continually making the choice to come back, every moment of every single day." – STEPHENIE ZAMORA

You may quickly realize after the death of a loved one that the day they died is not the hardest part. It may be the worst day of your life, but it is not the hardest part. The hardest part is returning to life again. Because while you had no say in your loved one's dying, you do have a say in your living. And choosing to live after someone you love has died is one of the hardest choices we make. It's okay if life after loss feels more like a struggle than the day your loved one died . . . because often, it is.

SEPTEMBER 8

USING visual objects to mark time is a common way grievers encourage themselves to live on after a loved one has died. Consider making a paper chain with 30 links representing 30 days. Each morning you wake up, or each night before you go to sleep, tear off a link and say, "I've made it another day." Repeat this process as often as you like to encourage yourself to continue living life after loss. You might also try this in reverse, beginning with one paper link and adding a new one every day for 30 days. It can be agonizing to see time passing, link by link, without your loved one here, but it's also a tangible way to remind yourself that you are capable of continuing and surviving at a time when going on seems impossible.

"When we share in each other's grief and pain, we lighten it. Or maybe we just give each other permission to feel it fully and, through that act of acceptance, the grief becomes more bearable. Because, like the rain, tears too have an end. And with deep emotions, we are open to each other in unexpected ways." – KARPOV KINRADE

Grief shared is grief lightened. In sharing our loss story with others, whether we simply speak our loved one's name or connect with their memory on a profound, deeper level, we shift from "I, and I alone, am carrying this" to "We are carrying this together." There is relief in being seen by someone else and knowing that they just get it.

SEPTEMBER 10

IF you're anything like me, you were raised to write thank-you notes every time you received something. Grief involves a lot of receiving, so sometimes it feels as if you're drowning in a sea of thank-yous that need writing. If the thought of cranking out thank-you notes is overwhelming, try shaking up the traditional thank-you. Send a short postcard with a beautiful illustration, repurpose memorial flowers by delivering them to a friend's porch, attach a photo of your loved one to an email and include your personal thanks in the text, or create one voice memo or video with a "blanket thank-you" and send it to everyone who contributed in some way. Or opt out of thank-you notes for the time being. At least for the first six months or so after a loss, friends and family will understand if you don't send them a personalized thank-you for bringing you a casserole when your loved one died.

SEPTEMBER 11

"Grief changes shape, but it never ends." – KEANU REEVES

Over the course of our lives, our grief becomes smaller and larger, wider and deeper, rounder and sharper, clearer and cloudier, lighter and darker. Grief is seasonal, just like we are. There are seasons when grief is especially loud, as if someone cranked up the volume on it, and there are seasons when it is especially quiet, as if it's taken a vacation for a little bit. Something that our grief never does, however, is end. It continues on and keeps us company in its own small/large, wide/deep, round/sharp, clear/cloudy, light/dark way.

SEPTEMBER 12

THE next time you interact with someone older than you, ask them about their grief. The older, the better! Senior citizens, veterans, and grand-parents almost always have some wisdom about grief and loss to share. Start the conversation by saying, "I lost my [insert relationship] recently. Could you tell me about a time when you had a big loss in your life?" Then, figuratively, sit at their feet and listen. Especially if the loss was long ago, observe how grief sticks with them today, and notice how they carry their grief now after years and years of carrying it. This older person may be able to serve as a model for how you'd like your grief to look in 10, 20, or even 30 years, and can help reassure you that while grief lives on, it's not intense and severe forever. If you're in an environment where older folks are scarce (such as a college campus or military base), check out the 20-20 Grief Project (2020griefproject.com), which features interviews with people looking back after 20 years of grieving a loss.

❝The most common reaction to loss is an inability to concentrate.❞ — RUSSELL FRIEDMAN AND JOHN W. JAMES

If you have trouble focusing in the wake of your loved one's death, you are not alone. Our brains respond to death by switching to "survival mode," and higher-level, thinking-heavy tasks like reading a stack of papers, having a deep conversation, or sitting through an hour-long meeting are often beyond our ability—at least for a little while. If you find yourself zoning out, take a deep breath and know there's nothing wrong with you or your brain; you're just grieving.

SEPTEMBER 14

ENLIST family, friends, coworkers, and neighbors to keep you on track in life after loss. For instance, when you're in conversation with a friend and they ask to meet again, say something like "I'm having trouble remembering dates lately. Can you text me tomorrow and remind me to follow up?" When you're struggling to be present in the company meeting, ask your coworker, "I think I know what we're getting at here, but can I paraphrase for you to make sure I have it right?" When you're on carpool duty every other week, say to your neighbor, "I think I'm on carpool duty this Monday. Is that what your calendar says?" Asking others to cross-check you can help you get grounded and nail down your focus at a time when it's prone to wander off.

SEPTEMBER 15

"Grief is an eraser." — GLENNON DOYLE

When someone we love dies, the future we imagined with them is totally erased. Our hopes, dreams, and expectations of "how life is supposed to be" fly right out the window, and blank, white emptiness takes their place. In grieving our loved one, we must also grieve our picture of the future. This does not mean your future is meaningless or filled with nothingness from here on out, but we must grieve our old dreams in order to make room for new ones—new ones forced into being by loss.

SEPTEMBER 16

PRACTICE grieving a dream by holding the experience of it in your mind and then watching it slowly dissolve like sugar in warm water. Close your eyes and picture a future experience you thought you were going to have with your loved one. This could be a milestone event like a wedding or a more intimate scene like sitting on the front porch together when you're old. Bring in all your senses. What do you see? What do you hear? What do you taste? What do you smell? What can you touch? Additionally, who is with you? Where are you? What are you wearing? What time of year is it? Really paint a picture of the scene. Know that it's okay to cry during this exercise. Hold the dream in your mind for a couple of minutes. Then, when you're ready, take a big, deep breath in and, as you exhale, watch the dream fade away. Just because this dream was only a picture in your mind doesn't make the loss of it any less valid than a real, tangible human loss. Come back to this exercise anytime you need to grieve the death of a dream.

" Mourning is not forgetting . . . It is an undoing. Every minute tie has to be untied and something permanent and valuable recovered and assimilated from the dust. The end is gain, of course. Blessed are they that mourn, for they shall be made strong, in fact. But the process is like all other human births, painful and long and dangerous." – MARGERY ALLINGHAM

There's a societal expectation that the grief process can be sped up, slowed down, or even fully completed. In reality, we grieve for as long as we live, and grief changes form over time. We can't snap our fingers and be done grieving. It's a continual process, like washing, folding, and storing a never-ending pile of laundry. As we grow and learn and change, new clothes are added to the pile, well-worn items are patched and mended with fresh thread, and special, treasured pieces get even more gentle treatment.

SEPTEMBER 18

I once had a client compare integrating grief into her life with making pastry dough. It takes time to combine all the ingredients, but it also takes work, practice, and focus on the task. Consider cooking or baking to cope with your grief. Hearty, comforting soups and stews that need time to simmer can remind you that there is no such thing as wasted time in grief; integration is happening whether you're "stirring the pot" or not! Beautiful baked goods can remind you that practice, not perfectionism, is the key to "getting it right." And foolproof toss-together recipes like pasta dishes and salads can remind you to keep experimenting; there's no one right way to grieve. See what parallels you can draw to grief in the kitchen—and nourish yourself in the process.

SEPTEMBER 19

"Acceptance asks only that you embrace
what's true." – CHERYL STRAYED

Acceptance is not about liking a situation; it's about recognizing that what happened did in fact happen and that circumstances cannot be changed or reversed. I will never ask you to like, love, or be grateful for the death of your loved one—that's wildly inappropriate and understandably impossible. What I will ask you to do is accept their death as a reality in your life and answer this question: "Given that the death of my loved one is a fact, where do I go from here?" Acceptance is not the final stage of grief; it is the beginning of stepping into your life after loss.

SEPTEMBER 20

JUST as grief doesn't happen all at once, neither does acceptance. Especially if you're in the first year or so of your grief, accepting what happened as fact can be particularly difficult. If saying the words "I accept their death as the truth" is hard for you, try "I'm beginning to accept their death is real" or "One day, I want to accept this with my whole heart" or "Eventually, I'll accept their death." Framing acceptance as a future event instead of a present pressure can help you ease up on the hurry to accept it and move on. Allow acceptance to happen on your time frame.

"Grief is like the ocean. It comes in waves, ebbing and flowing. Sometimes the water is calm and sometimes it's overwhelming. All we can do is learn to swim." – VICKI GARRISON

Do you feel as if you've been tossed into the middle of the sea without a life preserver? You're not alone. While we can logically understand the experience of grief, we don't really get it until we're grieving ourselves. And unfortunately, "getting it" looks a lot like floundering around in the middle of the ocean, learning to swim when we've never swum before. It's trial by fire, and it is often overwhelming. Nobody does grief well at first, and that's normal. Gradually, we learn to swim, and thankfully, we end up meeting others doing the doggy paddle of grief in the big, wide ocean with us.

IN the aftermath of loss, it's tempting to convince ourselves we're bad at life because we're not grieving perfectly. When you feel like you're failing at grief, practice something you *know*, beyond a shadow of a doubt, you're good at. This could be a creative pursuit like drawing, dancing, or playing an instrument, but it could also be a practical task, like masterfully unloading and reloading the dishwasher, organizing the family's budget, or making a needed repair on the car. What do friends and family say you're best at? What do coworkers admire you for? What comes easiest to you? While coming back from the loss of your loved one, lean on those abilities to remind yourself that even in the midst of loss, you're more than competent.

SEPTEMBER 23

"Death is not the opposite of life, but a part of it." — HARUKI MURAKAMI

Especially in Westernized society, there's a toxic narrative that equates death with failure, punishment, and negativity. Death = bad; life = good. We frame death as a failure to "win" against a disease or diagnosis, we punish wrongdoers with the death penalty, and we sell and market ways to prolong life via workouts, diet plans, and medications. However, death is woven into life, just like birth is woven into life. When we fold death into the experience of life, instead of making it life's adversary, we are able to see it as a normal experience that happens, instead of an awful nightmare that is brought upon us by some malevolent force. Death is not a failure to live; it is a natural occurrence knitted into every single one of our lives.

SEPTEMBER 24

YOU can help yourself normalize death as a natural occurrence by looking for signs of death all around you. When walking outside, observe flowers fading from bloom, leaves dropping from trees, and the remains of small animals that have died, such as birds and squirrels. Notice when businesses shutter their windows, cars are left to rust, and streetlights burn out. These are deaths, in some small way, and they can help you remember that not everything is bright and vibrant and pulsing all the time. Death is a part of life, and is integrated into every day.

" You have to love. You have to feel. It is the reason you are here on earth. You are here to risk your heart." – LOUISE ERDRICH

While numbness is often one of the first experiences grievers have after the loss of a loved one, some grieving people choose to adopt numbness for the long term—using it to dull the pain of their loss, but also the joy and connection of love. It can be tempting to use numbness to shield yourself from feeling grief, but you'll soon find that love is blocked out, too. When you sense yourself numbing out, allow yourself to come back to the world—a world that contains heartbreaking pain, yes, but also heart-mending love.

SEPTEMBER 26

WHEN we can't define emotions with words, it can be helpful to define them with feelings. The next time you're grappling with an intense emotion you just can't seem to put your finger on, close your eyes and ask yourself, "Where am I feeling this emotion in my body? Does this emotion have a temperature, weight, or texture? Is there pain associated with this emotion? If so, what kind" (for example, stabbing, scratching, ripping, throbbing)? Then allow yourself to fully feel and take in the bodily sensations of that emotion. Letting yourself feel emotion and notice it helps you digest it and release it from your body so that a different emotion can take its place. You may not know what anger feels like in the aftermath of loss, but you sure can zero in on "that tingly, burning feeling at the base of your skull."

SEPTEMBER 27

"And once the storm is over you won't remember how you made it through, how you managed to survive. You won't even be sure, in fact, whether the storm is really over. But one thing is certain. When you come out of the storm, you won't be the same person who walked in." – HARUKI MURAKAMI

You are not required to be the same person you were pre-loss. In fact, it's impossible for you to be. The person you are now is someone who has seen, known, and wholeheartedly experienced the life-changing loss of a loved one. That fact alone is reason enough for you to have changed. Release the pressure to hold on to the same habits, personality traits, preferences, and behaviors of your "old self." Loss has made it so that they can't all come along with you—and that's okay.

SEPTEMBER 28

ALMOST everyone who has ever grieved can point to something they miss about their old self. I miss my never-ending energy. In the aftermath of my mom's death, I found myself needing to take breaks and rest more than I used to. I had to grieve my 21-year-old self, the young woman with boundless energy and enthusiasm. Some days, I still do. The next time you're journaling, try to identify a trait you miss about your old self and allow yourself to grieve it. For instance, "Today, I miss my belief that the good guys always win," "Today, I miss my ability to do quick math in my head," "Today, I miss my habit of getting up at five a.m. sharp." Grant yourself permission to mourn the person you no longer are. Your old self is considered a loss, too.

" When we lose people we love, we don't mourn the past – we mourn un-lived tomorrows. We mourn the loss of people who knew us thoroughly and loved us anyway, and future memories that will never be made." – JAMES RUSSELL LINGERFELT

I'll admit it: It's hard to create, build, and maintain relationships with people who know all sides of you and love you anyway. Not everyone in your circle is your "person." And when you lose someone, especially your "person," it can feel like you'll never have another "person" ever again. There is grief for their life, absolutely, but there is also grief for the deep, intimate connection the two of you shared. Your relationship was special, and that's worth grieving.

SOMETIMES it can feel too painful to participate in an activity that you and your loved one were supposed to do together, and that makes perfect sense in the aftermath of loss. But consider this: participating in that activity might also trigger *happy* memories of your loved one. Start by doing a small activity that the two of you used to do together—going to the coffee shop for your classic Saturday-morning bagel and newspaper, for instance. Breathe deeply and see what memories you can draw on while you're there. Rest assured that you can go home whenever you'd like. Taking all the time you need, work your way up to larger and larger activities—dinners out, concerts, visits with family or friends, weeklong vacations. As you build up your emotional tolerance to places and spaces you were supposed to inhabit with your loved one, you may start noticing positive memories of them everywhere.

OCTOBER 1

" The belief that a person can and should only feel grief over one sad event at a time is a truly disturbing estimate of our emotional capacity." – JENNIFER ARMINTROUT

It comes as a shock to some grievers that they can feel more than one emotion at once. Whether they've never had an experience as complicated or as layered as grief or they simply didn't believe it was possible, they quickly learn that emotions can come in pairs, triplets, or even a tsunami. Those who have already felt more than one emotion at once know what it's like to swing wildly between an onslaught of emotions. Take comfort in the knowledge that you and your emotions are layered, just like your grief. It's okay—in fact, it's downright human—to feel more than one emotion at a time.

OCTOBER 2

ONE especially helpful modality for unlocking grief is nonverbal treatment, during which you are not required to put words to your emotions but simply to feel them. Body-based treatments such as Reiki, massage, and acupuncture are opportunities to receive care without needing to speak. When you sign up for a session, let your practitioner know that you've had a hard time lately and that it would be extra soothing if you closed your eyes and got lost in your thoughts during the treatment. Most practitioners are more than happy to do their work while allowing you mental and emotional space. As you receive treatment, concentrate on what it feels like to be focused on and tended to, and see if you can picture yourself healing in the presence of your practitioner.

"Most people are illiterate in the language of grief." – NORA MCINERNY

I often joke, "Not everybody knows what to do with me," and I'll bet the same is true for you. It's not that your friends and family don't love you or want to help you; it's that they don't know the language of grief. It may be true that everybody is doing everything they can to understand and support you, but not everything helps. On days like these, remember that you are not alone; everyone who has ever grieved knows what it's like to be in your shoes.

ANONYMITY becomes a strange kind of luxury after the death of a loved one. Try visiting a place that is full of people but where no one knows you, like a theme park, movie theater, art show, or neighboring town's farmers' market. Being in a space where no one knows you or your grief story can be a refreshing reminder that your loss isn't your entire identity, and that you do not have to make your loss story available to everyone. Sometimes it's okay to want to keep your grief hidden under the surface.

OCTOBER 5

"The people you love become ghosts inside of you and like this you keep them alive." – ROBERT MONTGOMERY

When someone we love dies, we hold our memory of them inside us. While we cannot be with their physical body, their presence lives on in our mind, heart, and spirit. We keep them alive through our thoughts and actions and honor them by remembering and celebrating who they were to us. There's no way we can ever forget our loved one; they are a permanent part of us.

OCTOBER 6

A fun, lighthearted way to keep your loved one alive in spirit is to pursue something they loved and embody their delight and enthusiasm in your own body. For instance, if your loved one was into bird watching, open one of their bird-watching books and see what colorful birds you can spot. If your loved one couldn't stop reading romance novels, pick one up and pretend you're experiencing the story through their eyes. If your loved one adored fixing motorcycles, take a motorcycle repair course and pretend your loved one is there teaching you a new skill. The point of pursuing an activity your loved one appreciated is not to be good at it, but to see if you can uncover the joy and passion they derived from it. It might help you feel connected to them and see a little more of what they saw in life.

"It has been said that "time heals all wounds." I do not agree. The wounds remain. In time, the mind, protecting its sanity, covers them with scar tissue and the pain lessens. But it is never gone." – ROSE FITZGERALD KENNEDY

If you're looking for an end to grief or a complete removal of grief from your life, good luck. I've yet to meet a grieving person in any moment of their grief journey who wasn't in some way continuing to grieve the death of their loved one. Time is powerful, but it does not have the power to heal; it merely has the potential to allow us more opportunities to practice living life without our loved one. The wound seals over, but the scar never disappears.

JUST about everyone who grieves has a dream of their loved one at one time or another. These dreams take all forms, from soft, lighthearted visitations to vivid, panic-inducing flashbacks to bizarre, silly happenstances. If you would like to see your loved one more often in your dreams, try writing your dreams down in a journal for 30 days. The moment you wake up, set a timer for 10 minutes and record everything from your dream that you remember. Doing so triggers your brain to recognize that you are paying attention to your dreams, and gradually, your brain will learn to provide you with more focus and recall in the morning. If you can't remember your dream or know you didn't dream, simply write, "I didn't have a dream last night," and wait to have a dream the next time you sleep. You can find out more about grief dreams and listen to the grief dreams of others at griefdreams.ca.

OCTOBER 9

"Grief and resilience live together." – MICHELLE OBAMA

Before the death of my mother, I was lukewarm toward stories of resilience and a life after the very worst has happened. But after my mom died, I gobbled up resilience stories like a gluttonous toddler, constantly keeping my eyes and ears peeled for opportunities to consume more. I craved proof that others were still standing and had somehow made it to the other side of their loss. I fed on their hope—at the time, I had none of my own—and I learned that resilience is not the cure for grief; grief and resilience live side by side.

OCTOBER 10

MANY grievers say they want to heal, but just like grief, the experience of healing is unique to each person. Your definition of healing and someone else's definition of healing may not be the same. So, ask yourself, "What does it mean for *me* to heal?" For instance, one of my clients said, "Healing for me is making deep connections with others again." Another wrote, "Healing for me is feeling like I have power over my grief; not the other way around." Mine is: "Healing for me is seeing the color in the world again, and being able to feel genuinely joyful about it." Knowing what it means for *you* to heal can help you set goals surrounding your grief and bypass goals that may not be a good fit. You can't heal with someone else's criteria. You decide what healing means to you.

"I used to be afraid that if I experienced grief it would overcome me and I wouldn't be able to survive the flood of it, that if I actually felt it I wouldn't be able to get back up. It's taught me that I can feel it and it won't swallow me whole." – ELISABETH KÜBLER-ROSS

Grief pushes us to the limits of our emotions, so it makes a lot of sense that we often feel as if grief will literally kill us or permanently incapacitate us. But allowing ourselves to engage with grief, even for 5 or 10 minutes at a time, teaches us that we are just a little bit larger than grief is. We can hold grief in our bodies, hearts, and minds without dying. We can be in the muck of our hard emotions . . . and remain standing.

SOME people treat doing grief work like an all-or-nothing, move-it-or-lose-it, you're-in-or-you're-out undertaking—as if the only way to grieve properly were to go all in and stay there. But you do not have to constantly grieve in order to process your grief effectively. Try giving grief little five-minute pockets of time in your day. Set a timer, close your eyes, and allow yourself to really *feel* the devastation, heartbreak, and loss. Go all the way in and let the pain and emotions wash over you. When the timer goes off, don't jump into a new task. Take a moment to wiggle your toes and fingers, slowly open your eyes, and feel your body wherever it is. Take a deep breath, thank yourself for being able to "go there," and then resume your day. Practicing grief in this way can help you move the emotions around it without feeling completely overwhelmed.

OCTOBER 13

" Freeing yourself was one thing, claiming ownership
of that freed self was another." – TONI MORRISON

There's a big difference between living life after loss and identifying as a
person who's living life after loss. One is an action, a series of routines and
motions; the other is an identity, a wholehearted "taking on" of your story.
When you take on the identity of a person who's living life after loss, you
acknowledge the fact not only that you're grieving, but also that you are a
grieving person who is allowing that truth to sink into your bones.

OCTOBER 14

BE your own cheerleader in life after loss. Whenever you pass yourself in
a mirror or see your reflection in a window, say to yourself, "I'm rooting for
you," "I have faith in you," or "I've got you." These small, simple phrases help
you both acknowledge yourself as a grieving person and, simultaneously,
recognize that you are your own ally in this new experience. Especially
when you're sad or scared, meeting your eyes in the mirror and uttering the
phrase "We're gonna make it through this together" is intensely powerful.

"The bravest thing I ever did was continuing my life when I wanted to die." – JULIETTE LEWIS

Life after loss can be dark and overwhelming, and just about everyone who's ever grieved has abstractly or momentarily considered taking their own life. Often, this impulse is not rooted in an actual desire to die. It's more a feeling of "If I didn't wake up tomorrow, that would be okay." If you're feeling this way, know that you are not alone. You can find help right now by texting "HOME" to the Crisis Text Line at 741-741, or contact the National Suicide Prevention Lifeline at 1-800-273-8255. (I have both these numbers saved in my phone.)

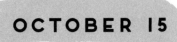

OCTOBER 16

ONE sneaky way to trick yourself into continuing to live your life after someone you love has died is to plan an event to look forward to. This could be something as big as a hot-air balloon ride or as small as a visit to your hairdresser. Whatever the event, it should be something you consider luxurious, a treat or a special indulgence. Don't make it something you feel you "have" to do, and definitely don't base it on someone else's idea of luxury. This should be something *you* want to experience. After the event has passed, schedule another event to look forward to, and keep encouraging yourself to live on. You may not see it now, but there is a lot in your life to look forward to—even if you have to manufacture that anticipation yourself.

OCTOBER 17

"Loss gets integrated, not overcome." – MEGAN DEVINE

I like to picture life as a tapestry being woven on a giant loom. When our loved one dies, it's as if some mysterious force added a new thread to the loom and grief is woven into our lives alongside everything else we had going for us. The death of our loved one becomes a part of who we are, not a part of us we're constantly trying to get rid of. Life after loss looks like integration, not elimination.

OCTOBER 18

IN the aftermath of my mom's death, I found myself making friends and connections that reminded me of her. I didn't purposely seek them out, but I noticed that many of the people I chose to spend time with immediately after she died were her age, her height, of her faith, or had her hair color. Of course, nobody could've replaced my mom in my life, but being around people who expressed her traits was comforting—and once I noticed the connection, I laughed. Now, when I make a new friend, I try to find a piece of my mom somewhere in them. See if you can surround yourself with people who remind you physically, emotionally, or spiritually of your loved one. You might just find some glimmers of your loved one in your new friend.

"I don't know what the hell is going on, and that's okay." – MARTHA BECK

Do you feel like you don't have a handle on anything? That's normal! When someone we love dies, we lose our sense of control and order. Everything—even something as simple as taking out the trash—can feel strange and foreign in the aftermath of loss. When you're feeling crazy, confused, and disoriented, know that there's nothing the matter with you; this experience is a part of grief.

WE need the world to feel safe and steady before we really go deep with our grief. If you find yourself putting off your grief, look around. Is your work life solid? How about your home life, your finances, your relationships, your health? If any of these feels out of control, you might not be able to take on the task of deep grief right now. I've met grievers who don't feel ready to do the work of grief until two, five, or even 10 years out from the death of their loved one. And each of their experiences is okay. Give yourself permission to get into a comfortable routine in most areas of your life before spelunking into the great depth of your loss. Your life doesn't have to be perfect for you to engage with grief, but it should feel reasonably safe before you take the plunge. It's okay to put off grief temporarily to secure your foundation.

OCTOBER 21

"Grief is characterized much more by waves of feeling
that lessen and reoccur, it's less like stages and more
like different states of feeling." – MEGHAN O'ROURKE

There is no linear way out of grief, and life after loss is not an event with a
finish line. While you may notice recurring themes or experiences in your
grief, they don't always appear in order, and they don't always make sense
to your brain. Grief is more like a zigzagging mountain trail than a line on a
graph. It's a mix of uphill and downhill paths, with some switchbacks tossed
in for good measure. Know that it's okay to feel like you're "back at square
one," because in grief, there are no squares at all.

OCTOBER 22

ENGAGING in grounding practices can help you feel rooted in the midst
of the changing emotions and feelings of grief, and a wonderful way to feel
grounded is to literally put your feet on the ground. I don't mean simply
walking. I mean taking off your shoes and socks and standing barefoot
in grass, moss, sand, or dirt. This practice, known as nature immersion,
earthing, or forest bathing, can remind you that you are safe and sound and
anchored at a time when you feel untethered from everything. Next time
you're walking outside, see if you can stop at a beach, park, soccer field, or
garden and practice literal grounding.

"I think you have to deal with grief in the sense that you have to recognize that you have it, and say that it's OK to have all the sadness." – ANN RICHARDS

The first step in coping with grief is recognizing that it's there in the first place. When you're feeling stressed, overwhelmed, or at your limit, consider that what you're experiencing might be grief. Saying something like "Ah! It's grief again" can give you space to feel all your emotions. It's okay to get a visit from grief, but sometimes you need to say hello to it first.

OCTOBER 24

TRY giving grief a name so you can greet it (or curse it) when it appears over and over again. I once had a client who named her grief "Kevin." Every time she felt something difficult or overwhelming, she'd say, "And here comes Kevin again, with the complicated emotions!" We both laughed and noticed that treating grief like an unwelcome visitor or an obnoxious neighbor helped her turn toward her grief instead of away from it. If your grief had a name, what would it be?

OCTOBER 25

"There comes a day when you smile again, and you feel like a traitor. How dare I feel happy. How dare I be glad in a world where my father is no more. And then you cry fresh tears . . . because giving up your grief is another kind of death." – LAURELL K. HAMILTON

Sometimes, there is security and foundation in fiercely holding on to our grief. But then a day comes when we're not actively grieving, when we're able to smile or sing or even laugh—and we wonder if we still miss our loved one, if we're still mourning their death, if we're still not okay without them here. The answer is "Of course." *Of course* you still miss your loved one. *Of course* you are still mourning their death. And *of course* you're still not okay without them here. The difference is that you have learned to feel things other than heartbreak, and these happier emotions are making themselves known to you. Joy does not cancel out grief. The two go hand in hand.

OCTOBER 26

I like to picture grief as a pair of bowls, one balanced in each hand. In one bowl, there is the death of my mother, the absolute worst thing that has ever happened to me. In the other bowl, there is the joy of being alive—the beautiful people and things I've seen and known and the knowledge that being alive on Earth is a glorious gift. One bowl is not heavier than the other; the two cannot possibly be weighed or compared. Life after loss means carrying both bowls with you wherever you go—grief in one hand, joy in the other. They can't cancel each other out, and they don't need to. There is room in me—and in you, too—to balance the two together.

" Hope is a revolutionary patience."

— ANNE LAMOTT

Hope is often framed as optimism, but I like to think of it more as endurance. To hope is to believe that the future might look different from how things look right now. Sometimes that hope looks a lot like a mix of faith and waiting. Each day you live life after loss is another opportunity to exercise your muscle of hope.

OCTOBER 28

LIFE after someone you love dies can be incredibly lonely. There's an ache to "hear from" your lost loved one, to know that they're safe and okay, and to reassure yourself that they continue to be with you in some way. If you're struggling to "feel" or "see" your loved one after their death, try assigning them a symbol. Birds, butterflies, flowers, songs, numbers, cars—anything is up for grabs! Whenever you see that symbol, greet it as you would have greeted your loved one, and remember something you loved about them. For instance, when I see sparrows, I say, "Hey, Mom," and take a moment to remember her embrace. Whether you believe your loved one is sending you these signs or you know you're inventing them yourself, the outcome is the same: a moment of hope and connection with your loved one.

OCTOBER 29

"Just because you're scarred for life doesn't mean
you should be scared to live." – BRIAN CELIO

Our brains are designed to shield us from pain, and experiencing a devastating loss can make us understandably afraid of living life. After all, the death of a loved one shows us that we live in a world where *anything* can happen. How is that not (even a little bit) scary? It's okay to be scared of living life after loss, but as much as you can, don't allow fear to have the final say. Your scars are more than evidence that you've been wounded. They are also proof that you are still alive.

OCTOBER 30

IT may be helpful to prepare for grief triggers in the aftermath of a loved one's death. Whether you're getting ready to watch a movie with friends and family or trick-or-treating in your neighborhood on Halloween, it's okay to ask if you should expect something dark or scary. Consider saying something like "I've had a hard time with death scenes since I lost [loved one]. Does anybody die in this movie?" or "Are the Richardsons decorating for Halloween this year? I don't think I'm ready to handle anything with coffins or caskets just yet." This simple request is a small way to offer yourself a little love and protection at a time when you're feeling fragile. It's okay to opt out of an experience or activity if you think it might be triggering for you. There's no shame in delegating yourself to "doorbell duty" on Halloween night.

" To succeed, you have to do something and be very bad at it for a while. You have to look bad before you can look really good." – BARBARA DEANGELIS

Grief is often clunky, clumsy, and awkward. It's a frustrating combination of "death is taboo to talk about" and "doing grief for the first time," and that can make you self-conscious about how you look as a griever. Take heart and know that each awkward experience you have is a step toward your growth. You are learning how to do life with grief, and it's more than okay to be (and feel like) a beginner.

NOVEMBER 1

YOU might be surprised by the plethora of odd resources available about grief and loss. Try Googling random combinations, like "grief dance" or "grief and cats," and see what comes up. If you can imagine it, there's probably an article, video, or podcast about it online. (One of my personal favorites is "grief flowers," and I spent an afternoon reading up on the historical symbolism behind sympathy flowers.) Bookmark or save websites that resonate with you, creating a comforting file of unique-to-you grief resources. It's one more way to show yourself that there's no one right way to grieve and that grief shows up in all kinds of places.

NOVEMBER 2

"Healing requires taking action. It is not a passive event." – CAROLINE MYSS

In order to heal from the death of a loved one, we must *do something*. Starting off in a direction, any direction, helps us get our bearings and reorient ourselves to life after loss. Even if we discover that the direction we're heading in is a dead end, we now know which way *not* to go. Pick something to do in the aftermath of loss and *just do it*. Healing happens along the way.

NOVEMBER 3

ISOLATION is the experience most commonly reported by grievers. In the wake of the death of a loved one, it's normal to feel cut off from friends and family who don't understand, and it's okay to be angry at people who have distanced themselves from you. But be careful not to write off your loved ones too quickly. Many people want to help but may not know exactly how you *want* to be helped. Perhaps they need a nudge from you before stepping in and offering support. Simply put: your friends and family can't read your mind. If you're feeling ignored or unsupported, reach out. Send a text or pick up the phone. If you're not sure what to ask for, try something small, like "I'm feeling rough tonight. Want to go for a walk?" or "I'm having a hard day. Is it okay if we sit on the phone together without speaking?" or "I'm not doing well. Can I come over and hang out on your couch?" Believe that people want to be there for you, because more often than not, they sincerely do.

"Grief doesn't have a plot. It isn't smooth. There is no beginning and middle and end." – ANN HOOD

Grief is less like a predictable sequence and more like an amorphous blob of uncertainty. You can't forecast your way out of grief, because there's no way to determine when the next wave is coming. This may seem disheartening at first, but when you recognize that there is no structure for grief, you can stop trying to pinpoint exactly where you are on your journey. If there's no road map, it's impossible to be lost.

IF journaling is tricky for you, consider writing a letter as if you were updating your loved one on your life. Start with "Dear [loved one's name]," and then share with them your daily experiences, inner thoughts, and future plans. Get creative if you like and enclose photos or mementos from your life after loss. You may find that after some time, you no longer need to write directly to your loved one and can journal freely. Or—and this is okay, too— continue writing as if you were corresponding directly with your loved one.

NOVEMBER 6

"Strength doesn't come from what you can do. It comes from overcoming the things you once thought you couldn't." – RIKKI ROGERS

At first, there is an air of impossibility to grief. How are we supposed to live in a world where our loved one is dead? It doesn't seem doable. But we continue living, slowly and reluctantly in the first days and weeks, and then, with patience and practice, ever more surely and confidently as time goes on. We find that we are strong—not because we summoned strength from thin air, but because we grew it inside ourselves one day at a time.

NOVEMBER 7

WHILE many of our hopes and dreams are extinguished by the death of a loved one, sometimes we still have dreams for the future. Initially, you may feel like your desire to go after your dreams is gone, and that's to be expected. But try this: Somewhere private and safe, keep a list of the things you dream of doing someday. The list doesn't have to be long, and your dreams don't have to be profound. Aim to have at least three items on it. Then tuck the list securely away. Set a calendar reminder to return to it in a year. After a year has passed, you may find that you have inadvertently accomplished some of your dreams or that your desire to pursue them has returned. It's a little reminder that your dreams aren't permanently gone; they're just waiting for you to return to them.

NOVEMBER 8

" Healing is not about moving on or 'getting over it,' it's about learning to make peace with our pain and finding purpose in our lives again." – SHIRLEY KAMISKY

Grief is not a game that is won or lost; it's an experience in which, every day, you try, as much as you can, to be a little better than you were the day before. Even if you're not measurably "happier," growth can also look like mindful awareness and self-compassion. The goal of grief isn't to get past it, but to make a place for it in the larger picture of your life.

NOVEMBER 9

WHEN most people think of grief support groups, they think of metal folding chairs circled around boxes of tissues, and yes, there is absolutely something to be said for the power of in-person grief support. But if you're not feeling social or you want to practice being vulnerable before taking your grief out into the world, consider searching for a grief support course online. There are all kinds of grief support courses, including interactive courses, where you can connect to a group of fellow grievers through chat or video, and more hands-off courses, where you can go at your own pace without collaboration or input from others. Try Googling "online grief support course" or "virtual grief support course" to see what's available now.

NOVEMBER 10

"It's funny how, even long after you've accepted the grief of losing someone you love and truly have gotten on with your life . . . something comes up that plays 'gotcha,' and for a moment or two the scar tissue separates and the wound is raw again." — MARY HIGGINS CLARK

Even if you haven't been formally diagnosed with PTSD, the loss of a loved one is traumatizing. Sights, scents, sounds, and even tastes can send us right back to the very worst moments of our lives, and it's intensely jarring to live life in anticipation of the next trigger. In addition to working with a mental health professional, it can be helpful to remember that you are not being triggered because you're weak or incapable. It's because you've lived through something really, really hard. And that's the exact opposite of weakness.

NOVEMBER 11

WHILE it's normal to be triggered after someone you love dies, it can be debilitating to feel like you're constantly under attack. If you feel safe doing so, brainstorm small ways to expose yourself to your triggers so you can gradually come into close contact with them in the future. For instance, after my mom died, I could barely stand to see mothers and daughters out in public. I knew I didn't want this to be my new reality, so I gradually started reacquainting myself with mothers and daughters. First, I would observe mother-daughter pairs as I walked. Then, I purposely got in line behind mother-daughter pairs at the grocery store. And then, I made a point of going out on holidays like Mother's Day. Now, I still feel a twinge of heartache when I see a mom with her daughter, but the urge to scream is gone.

" I don't think grief is a price we pay for love, but rather that it is a part of love. When death comes, I think the grief is to be experienced the way joy was experienced before – and if we experience it intimately, grief and joy are not separate, and both are love." – BARRY GRAHAM

What if grief is not a consequence of love but another *expression* of it? What if our deep sorrow is a reflection of deep connection? There is no grief without attachment, investment, and some kind of emotional bond. The fact that we grieve is evidence of how completely we are able to love.

SOMETHING about musical and tonal sound unlocks emotions in a way that words cannot. If you're struggling to put your grief into words or want to experience an activity in which you're not required to articulate your grief, try a sound meditation or "sound bath." Most sound baths feature a combination of gongs, singing bowls, bells, and vocal tones that are intended to suspend you in a safe place of mental, emotional, and possibly spiritual exploration. Even if you don't have the energy to go deep into your psyche (because that's difficult sometimes in grief), try resting your eyes as you sit in a chair or lie on the floor listening. Sound baths can be found both in person and online.

NOVEMBER 14

"No matter how bleak or menacing a situation may appear, it does not entirely own us. It can't take away our freedom to respond, our power to take action." – RYDER CARROLL

It's normal to feel hopeless in the aftermath of loss, but hopelessness is not the full story. Even in the direst situations, you have some measure of power and control over what you're thinking and what your physical body is doing. You may not be able to rearrange your outer circumstances to your liking, but you can claim power over your mind and your actions.

NOVEMBER 15

SOMETHING that you have a great deal of control over is how often you eat and drink in the aftermath of loss. As best you can, try to eat three to four meals and drink eight 8-ounce glasses of water per day. Doing so keeps your blood sugar from crashing and wards off unpleasant physical sensations like lightheadedness and racing heartbeat. If remembering to eat and drink is difficult for you, set alarms to keep you scheduled. There are also a host of apps that remind you to eat and drink. Your body will thank you for keeping it nourished and stable in the midst of grief.

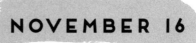

" Rock bottom became the solid foundation on which I rebuilt my life." – J. K. ROWLING

While rock bottom isn't the most pleasant place to live, it does have one redeeming quality: it's rock bottom. Anything that is different from rock bottom is an improvement on rock bottom—and in those small gains, there is hope. The death of your loved one is a solid, unchanging fact of which you can say, "That's the place where I was forced to start again." And in starting again, you are building your way up from rock bottom.

YOUNG adult literature, especially if it's fantastical or magical in nature, can be a marvelous tool for processing grief. Despite being written with kids in mind, series like *Harry Potter*, *The Chronicles of Narnia*, *His Dark Materials*, and the *Little House* books touch on themes of grief and loss while also exploring friendship, courage, and growing up. You might find inspiration and community in the stories of others working to face adversity while living rich, complicated lives.

NOVEMBER 18

" People you love never die . . . Not completely. They live in your mind, the way they always lived inside you. You keep their light alive. If you remember them well enough, they can still guide you, like the shine of long-extinguished stars could guide ships in unfamiliar waters." – MATT HAIG

Even though your loved one's body is no longer physically here, you are allowed to maintain an emotional, mental, and spiritual relationship with them. You are even allowed to change the boundaries of your relationship, such as how often you speak with them and the ways in which you communicate. Death ended your loved one's life, but your love for them and your need to include them in your own life live on.

NOVEMBER 19

AROUND the holidays, the presence of "the empty chair" that your loved one used to occupy can seem especially loud. If you're facing an empty chair at a holiday gathering this year, try honoring your loved one in a new way. Gather framed photos and set them at your loved one's traditional place at the table, invite guests to leave a note of love in their chair, place fresh flowers or a favorite stuffed animal where they would normally sit, or offer the empty chair to a friend or family member who might not have a place to go this holiday season. There's no such thing as replacing your loved one, but you always have the opportunity to honor them.

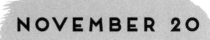

"I realized that it was not that I didn't want to go on without him. I did. It was just that I didn't know why I wanted to go on." – KAY REDFIELD JAMISON

After someone we love dies, we may lose our reason for living. We may recognize that we want to live, but it may feel like we're missing someone or something to live for. If you're searching for a "why" to live for, you are not alone. Many grievers know all too well the feeling of searching for a new purpose, new meaning.

NOVEMBER 21

MAKE a list of people, places, pets, things, experiences, dreams, and opportunities to live for. Individually, each item on your list may not fill you with purpose, but together, they create a life worth living. Instead of asking, "What gets me up in the morning?"—because in grief, the answer may be "Nothing"—ask, "What is worth staying up for?" We're not looking for motivation to stand up with this exercise; we're looking for what compels you to remain standing.

NOVEMBER 22

"Forgiveness is giving up the hope that the past could have been any different." — OPRAH WINFREY

When we forgive, we acknowledge that we and everyone else involved in the situation did the very best they could with the information, upbringing, tools, and circumstances they had at the time. We stop torturing ourselves for not knowing what we couldn't have known and set ourselves free from the impossible pressure of going back and making things different. When you forgive, you're not saying, "I'm okay with what happened." You're saying, "You tried your best . . . and so did I."

NOVEMBER 23

CLOSURE happens more in the movies and on TV than it does in real life. When someone we love dies, we are forced to manufacture our own kind of closure. That includes forgiving our loved one and ourselves for what was left unsaid and undone. If you're living with remorse, regret, or guilt, try this: Write down the regrets you need to release on bits of paper and then burn the paper safely in an ashtray or fireplace. Frame each regret like this: "I forgive you for [loved one's action]." If this is too difficult, or you don't feel 100 percent ready to forgive yet, try writing, "I want to forgive you for [loved one's action]." As you're writing and releasing these regrets, don't forget to include forgiveness for yourself. Start with blanket self-forgiveness, like "I forgive you for not knowing what you couldn't have known." Then, if it feels safe for you, get more specific. For example, "I forgive you for not taking time off of work to take care of Dad." Through forgiveness and self-forgiveness, you can create your own kind of closure.

" The reality is that you will grieve forever. You will not 'get over' the loss of a loved one; you will learn to live with it. You will heal and you will rebuild yourself around the loss you have suffered. You will be whole again but you will never be the same. Nor should you be the same nor would you want to." – ELISABETH KÜBLER-ROSS

Many grievers resent the fact that loss changes them, but for me, my evolution has been proof that my mom's death mattered and made an impact on my life. I cannot be who I was before because someone I loved a lot ceased to exist on this earth, and that's huge. It would be weirder if I hadn't changed at all. Everyone changes as a result of loss; it's okay that you aren't who you used to be.

NOVEMBER 25

SOMETHING many of my clients have found helpful is the mindful visualization of putting their old self to bed. Close your eyes and picture your pre-loss self in as much detail as you can. What do you look like? What are you wearing? How do you feel about your life? What are your hopes, dreams, and goals? Open your eyes. The next time you feel yourself judging your new self for not being the person your old self used to be, close your eyes and picture your new self walking your old self to bed and tucking them in. For added oomph, say something like "I know it's hard that I can't be you anymore, but I'm a different person now, and it's time for you to rest." This may help you release the grip your old self has on your new, grieving self.

NOVEMBER 26

"You may have to fight a battle more than once to win it." – MARGARET THATCHER

In order to get "good" at grief, you have to practice grieving over and over again. This does not mean being constantly sad, but actively engaging with grief each time it appears, instead of avoiding it or pushing it away. It can be frustrating at first, because most of us are not explicitly taught how to grieve, but gradually, we can learn to remain upright in the face of our grief and become "good" at dealing with it.

NOVEMBER 27

MEDITATION is an easy, portable way to get in touch with your grief. Whether you practice silent meditation or guided meditation, try sitting with your thoughts and feelings for five minutes per day, allowing them to surface, speak, and fade. At first, five minutes may feel like an eternity, but with time, focus, and practice, you can stretch your meditation sessions to 10 or 15 minutes per day. As you meditate, think about seeing yourself and your thoughts from an outsider's, or observer's, perspective. You may find that detaching yourself from your grief by one degree of separation can help you uncover valuable insights about and compassion for yourself.

"Even though I still felt a constant ache, I seemed
unknowingly to have traveled a little distance away from
that first unbearable pain. I sat up straighter and drew a
deep breath, and it was then that I began to believe that I
might really make my way through this." – ANNE TYLER

There comes a tipping point in everyone's grief journey when hope moves
from an abstract, far-off dream to a concrete, present thought. It's not
always the loudest or flashiest moment of your grief experience, but it's a
pivotal one, as it marks the instant you stop yearning for hope to appear and
realize it has finally arrived. It may not be big or grand or showy, but it is
there all the same. Hope is within your grasp at last.

NOVEMBER 29

USE deep breathing to steady yourself in the midst of loss. When you're
feeling anxious or overwhelmed, use "4-7-8 breathing": Tell yourself to
breathe, then actively suck in a giant breath of air for four seconds. Hold it
for seven seconds, then exhale for at least eight seconds. Repeat this pattern of breathing in and out until you feel yourself settling down. For extra
credit, focus your inhalation and exhalation on your lower belly instead
of your rib cage. Studies show that deep, diaphragm-based breathing can
soothe us faster than shallow, chest-centered breathing.

NOVEMBER 30

"Worrying is carrying tomorrow's load with today's strength – carrying two days at once. It is moving into tomorrow ahead of time. Worrying doesn't empty tomorrow of its sorrow, it empties today of its strength." – CORRIE TEN BOOM

Are you worried about your life after loss? You are not alone. When my mom died, I worried about everything, from whether I was going crazy to what everyone around me was thinking and feeling to what the heck my future would turn out to be now that the worst thing I could imagine happening had happened. While fear is useful at times, worry can set us spinning in circles at a time in our lives when we're already dizzy. It's normal to do a lot of worrying in life after loss, but at some point, it's worth asking yourself, "What does worrying do for me?"

DECEMBER 1

ONE of the very best tools I gave a client was the idea of a "future worries" list. If you're stressing about all the things you need to accomplish, manage, and take care of in the distant and *really* distant future, take out a piece of paper and write "Future Worries" at the top. Then write, "One day, I'll need to worry about . . ." and fill in the list with everything you know you'll have to address one day. These can be tasks like "selling the house," "taking care of our aging family members," and "writing a will." If the worry is about something that's going to happen more than a year from now, put it on the list. Releasing all your worries in one place can help you feel like you've done something with them. You may find that once you've written your worries down, they cease to be so loud. Anytime a future worry comes up, add it to your list.

"My scars remind me that I did indeed survive my deepest wounds. That in itself is an accomplishment. And they bring to mind something else, too. They remind me that the damage life has inflicted on me has, in many places, left me stronger and more resilient. What hurt me in the past has actually made me better equipped to face the present." – STEVE GOODIER

The fact that you are living life after loss is proof that you can survive loss. You don't need to be stronger, braver, or more capable to live life after loss; *you are already living it.* Know that while your scars are very real and very painful, they are evidence that you have made it and are making it through.

EXERCISE is a powerful way to boost your healing. If you feel ready to "work out" your grief, lace up your running shoes or hit the gym with a friend. Moving your body, even for 20 minutes a day, can help balance your mood, hormones, and stress levels. If high-intensity training is not doable, try low-impact sports like cycling, swimming, or yoga. As you exercise, be aware of your breath and take note of what it feels like to be in your body right now. Picture yourself working together with your body to keep you healthy and strong.

DECEMBER 4

" Feel. Grieve . . . Just sit and let it all rip you apart. And then get up and keep breathing. One breath at a time. One day at a time. Wake up, and be shredded. Cry for a while. Then stop crying and go about your day. You're not okay, but you're alive." — JASINDA WILDER

You don't have to be okay after someone you love dies. In fact, it's more than understandable if you're not. If you're struggling to feel okay, don't think about how you're going to survive the next 24 hours or even the next hour. Your only job is to take the next breath, the next step. It may feel silly to shrink your focus to the next moment after living day to day (or more) pre-loss, but loss changes how time works. It's normal to break the day down into tiny little pieces in order to survive.

DECEMBER 5

IF possible, find an isolated or remote place where you can express your grief vocally. Yelling, keening, shrieking, and shouting can help you tap into the harder, less explainable emotions of grief, like anger and despair. Sometimes, there aren't words to express grief, but there are sounds, and those sounds deserve to be let loose. While polite society isn't the most appropriate place to scream, there are locations (cornfields, forests, oceans) that are perfect for welcoming your wails. Note that if you're going somewhere alone, let a friend or family member know where you'll be and when you expect to arrive home.

" The grief doesn't go away . . . It's like carrying a heavy stone . . . you learn to settle the weight properly, and then you get used to it, and then sometimes you can forget you're carrying it." – RACHEL NEUMEIER

When someone you love dies, it's like a ginormous boulder has been added on top of the life you're already living. It's an instant burdening, a nonnegotiable weight placed on top of an already full life. Gradually, you find a place for the boulder, and your muscles get stronger and more agile. The big boulder of grief doesn't get any lighter, but you develop an ability to carry it with a little more flexibility and a little more ease.

DECEMBER 7

WHEN the burden of grief gets too heavy to bear, find a safe place to sit and close your eyes. Place your feet firmly on the ground. After taking a few deep breaths, picture a large bowl on the ground in front of you. Visualize your brain opening like a doorway and pouring its contents into the bowl. Keep breathing as you "brain-dump" into this big bowl. When everything is poured out, take another deep breath and picture your full bowl sinking into the ground like rainwater, taking its contents with it. Repeat this exercise anytime you're feeling overwhelmed or loaded down by the weight of loss.

DECEMBER 8

" With the new day comes new strength and new thoughts." — ELEANOR ROOSEVELT

While some of your thoughts might be the same from day to day, it's impossible to "think" the same day twice. Every morning you wake up is a chance to greet a day peppered with fresh thoughts. Whether you pursue these thoughts is up to you, but know that even when you feel like you're stuck in a rut, your thoughts say otherwise.

DECEMBER 9

ON a piece of paper, list the top 10 negative thoughts that run through your mind on a given day: "I'm never going to make it out of this," "I'm not as strong as I used to be," "This has ruined me," and so on. Then list the exact opposite of those 10 negative thoughts and pump them up with a positive or optimistic twist. For instance, the opposite of "I'm never going to make it out of this" might be "I'm going to make it out of this, and I will find joy along the way." The opposite of "I'm not as strong as I used to be" might be "I'm stronger than I used to be." And the opposite of "This has ruined me" might be "This has empowered me." See how it feels to think these thoughts. You don't have to believe them, but it may be helpful to introduce them to your collection of daily musings. Try this journaling prompt every day to add a counter perspective to your heaviest thoughts.

DECEMBER 10

"Our greatest glory is not in never falling, but in rising every time we fall." – CONFUCIUS

As much as we'd like to, it's impossible to live a life free from loss. If you're beating yourself up for falling, remember: no one escapes a fall (or falls). What matters is getting back up—not in a grand or super-heroic way, but in a persistent, insistent way that says, "I'm still here. I'm getting back up."

DECEMBER 11

ONE of my clients found pleasure in taking stock of her small wins. Once a day, she paused and thought of one thing she had accomplished. Then she wrote down that win in a journal. Eventually, she chose to share her small wins on social media so that her friends and family could cheer her on, too. Try keeping a record of a small win once per day. When you're selecting your daily entry, keep in mind that it may not be a conventional win by society's standards (trophies, medals, gold stars), but as long as it's an accomplishment for you, it's a win! Some of my favorites are: "Went for a walk even though it was raining," "Started singing in the shower again," and "Called tech support for help instead of giving up." See what small wins you observe in your own life after loss.

DECEMBER 12

" Though no one can go back and make a brand new start, anyone can start from now and make a brand new ending." – CARL BARD

While the death of your loved one has certainly crashed some of your future hopes and dreams, your future is not entirely lost. Your life is not over; life *as you knew it* is over. There is a small but important difference between the two. Because your life goes on, your future has the potential to be reimagined and remade . . . and the power to do so lies squarely with you.

DECEMBER 13

SOMETIMES it feels like all our friends and family want from us is the certainty of a happy, put-together future. We're peppered with questions like "When are you going to start dating again?" and "So, are you going back to school?" and "Will you have another kid then?" While it's clear they want us to be happy, it hurts to feel pushed into a future we're not sure of yet. When someone asks you about your future plans, try saying, "I'm doing my best to live each day as it comes. I see what you're getting at, but I'm not ready to jump that far ahead right now." See if this statement helps you lovingly set boundaries between you and those eager to gaze into the crystal ball of your future.

" They wrap [holidays] up all neatly with a turkey and clever gifts and lots of eggnog and laugh and laugh, but at the end of the day there are always people missing from the table. And you have to either sit with those empty chairs and laugh, or you can choose not to come to the table at all. I would rather come to the table." — JULIE BUXBAUM

I won't lie and tell you that the holidays are easy after someone you love dies. What I will tell you is that you have a choice about how you show up to the parties, the dinners, and the cookie swaps. You can zero in on the fact that your loved one is no longer here and operate solely from that head space or you can acknowledge your loved one's death and try your very best to find something to appreciate. If you look closely, you might be able to spot a glimpse of your loved one in the lights, the candles, the laughter, or the music.

DECEMBER 15

CONSULT with family members and friends about your holiday traditions. The death of your loved one has likely impacted all of you in a different way, and planning for the holidays might spare everyone unwanted conflict or hurt feelings. Get together as a group in person, via email, or over the phone and decide: Which traditions should stay the same? Which traditions need to be modified and in what ways? Which traditions should be discontinued? If you're overwhelmed by the thought of stopping a tradition altogether, try discontinuing it just for this year. As much as you're able, stay open-minded to new traditions or rituals that grow from the loss of your loved one.

DECEMBER 16

"The irony is that we attempt to disown our difficult stories to appear more whole or more acceptable, but our wholeness – even our wholeheartedness – actually depends on the integration of all of our experiences, including the falls." – BRENÉ BROWN

Sometimes, it feels like friends, family, and society want us to wear a mask instead of telling it like it is. The myth is that it's easier to pretend that everything is all right even though, behind the mask, everything is falling apart. While it feels like the mask might keep us from being on the receiving end of judgment and criticism, in reality, it just keeps us from engaging with our grief. Take a deep breath and start chipping away at your mask. The whole you deserves to be known and loved.

DECEMBER 17

IT'S not always safe to share our grief stories, but it's hard to tell which people are safe and which aren't. In the immediate aftermath of your loss, practice "unmasking" yourself in the presence of other grievers. When you feel ready, start to share with people in your life who are less familiar with grief how you're *really* doing. If you're not sure where to begin, say something like "The truth is, I'm feeling [insert emotion]." See how they respond. If they welcome you sans mask, consider them a safe place for your grief story and continue. If they attempt to make you feel better, it's okay to put on your mask again until you can make an excuse to remove yourself from the conversation. It takes some time to feel out your safe people in the aftermath of loss, but when you locate them, indulge in the freedom that comes with being yourself around them.

"Grief is forever. It doesn't go away; it becomes a part of you, step for step, breath for breath." – JANDY NELSON

Grief literally changes and rearranges the cells of our bodies. Our brains rewire, our nerves fire us up and settle us down, and our immune systems do everything they can to protect us from stress. When our loved one dies, our bodies feel it—from the immediate impact to the lasting effects. Grief leaves a visible and invisible impression on our lives, in our lungs, in our brains, and in our hearts. Everyone who has ever grieved is, at least partially, made up of grief.

DECEMBER 19

IF you find yourself holding stress in your body, try tensing all your muscles at once and then relaxing them one by one, starting with your feet and moving all the way up to your neck, jaw, and eyes. This is extraordinarily helpful anytime you're trying to go to sleep. Instead of focusing intensely on de-stressing one particularly tense part of your body, recruit your whole body to tense and untense together. In a strange and lovely way, it's a method of letting your body know that it's "all clear" and okay to fully relax.

DECEMBER 20

"There are people whose death leaves you with an ache of grief. A slight sting. And then there are people whose death stops time. Deaths that leave the sky murky all day long because even the sun is grieving. Deaths that shut down your muscles and stop the music." – PATRICIA AMARO

The only losses that can be realistically compared are your own losses against each other. It's impossible to measure the depth, grief, and impact of someone else's losses if you are not that person. Only you can decide which of your losses was the hardest and which the most powerful. Don't let anybody tell you that the death of your loved one was not significant enough, meaningful enough, or important enough for you to grieve. You and you alone have the power to determine exactly how much your loss matters. Only you know what it's like to be in your shoes.

DECEMBER 21

THE next time someone tries to compare losses with you, let them know you appreciate the fact that they're trying to empathize but you would rather they not measure their pain against yours. Say something like "I appreciate your sharing that with me, and I know you're just trying to help, but the death of [loved one's name] is really special and unique to me, and I'd like to avoid comparing them to anyone else." This soft but straightforward boundary is a helpful way of letting the other person know that you get their intention but that you would prefer a different approach.

" If you suddenly and unexpectedly feel joy, don't hesitate. Give in to it." – MARY OLIVER

Before loss, we never second-guess joy. We allow ourselves to have it and hold it. But after loss—when we've experienced the heartache of the death of a loved one—we are quick to be critical of joy. We're suspicious of it and wonder how long it will last before the other shoe drops down on our heads. It takes a lot of wherewithal to feel joy again in the midst of grief, but next time joy appears, give it a try. You might find you've been aching for it.

A little while ago, I came up with the 1 percent rule for grief. It goes like this: No matter how incredible your life is, no matter what you've achieved, no matter what luck/blessing/good fortune comes your way, your heart will always be composed of at least 1 percent grief. One percent of you will always remind you of the bittersweetness of a moment. One percent of you will always ache for your loved one to be present. One percent of you will never, ever forget the pain you've experienced in your life. I don't say this to discourage you. In fact, just the opposite: When you recognize that your heart will always be at least 1 percent grief, you can release the dream of feeling 100 percent joy and happiness. The next time you see joy heading your way, embrace it, knowing that some small part of you will continue to grieve. When this happens, try saying, "There's that pesky one percent again!"

DECEMBER 24

"In the midst of winter, I found there was, within me, an invincible summer. And that makes me happy. For it says that no matter how hard the world pushes against me, within me, there's something stronger – something better, pushing right back." – ALBERT CAMUS

Some days, it feels like grief has all the power and could swallow us up in its darkness at any minute. But what if there were something in us that was brighter and louder than the despair brought on by loss? In everyone who grieves, there is something that endures, an invincible summer that continues on, even in the midst of the harshest winter.

DECEMBER 25

SIT in a chair with both feet on the floor and close your eyes. Take a few deep breaths to center yourself and ground yourself in the present. Picture grief in front of you. What does it look like, feel like, sound like, and taste like? Form a clear picture of the size, shape, texture, and movement of grief in your mind. Then picture yourself growing larger and larger and larger, until you're able to swallow grief whole like a vitamin or a piece of candy. Feel it settling inside you alongside your beating heart, your breathing lungs, your churning mind. Continue breathing as you allow the bigness that is you to absorb and soak up the experience of grief. Then open your eyes and return to the present. Come back to this visualization anytime your grief feels larger than life.

"I wasn't prepared for the fact that grief is so unpredictable.
It wasn't just sadness, and it wasn't linear. Somehow
I'd thought that the first days would be the worst and
then it would get steadily better – like getting over the
flu. That's not how it was." – MEGHAN O'ROURKE

Grief sometimes feels like you're a lone little pinball, bouncing around
uncontrollably inside a wildly unpredictable pinball machine. One minute
it's rage, the next it's nostalgia. Round and round and round she goes! Grief
is less like the flu and more like a finicky knee. Who knows why it's acting
up? It could be the weather or it could be that you've been standing on it too
long. If you're struggling to find a logical pattern in the midst of grief, you
are not alone. Life after loss is a wild ride, and an often unpredictable one
at that.

ONE of the most helpful things another grief writer shared with me is this:
You don't have to know exactly what emotion you're feeling. You just have
to feel it. Sometimes, we put so much pressure on ourselves to get to the
root of what we're feeling that we forget to feel it in the first place. The next
time you're face-to-face with an unpleasant emotion, especially if it's your
first time feeling it, try sitting with it for a minute or two before rushing to
name it. It can be difficult, retraining your grief to enter your heart before it
enters your head, but it can help you to slow down and remember that grief is
an emotional experience to be had, not a logical experience to figure out.

DECEMBER 28

" The dead can survive as a part of the lives of
those that still live." – KENZABURŌ ŌE

When someone you love dies, you get the final say on how much space their presence occupies in your life. Of course, they don't leave your mind for a second, but how much of your time would you like to devote to honoring their memory and celebrating their life? What rituals, practices, and traditions would you like to perform in their absence? You are the conductor of the choir that is your life. What notes will your loved one sing?

DECEMBER 29

BEFORE stepping into the New Year, take an hour or so to list the year's upcoming griefiversaries and make a loose plan for how you would like to commemorate each one. Birthdays, anniversaries, deathiversaries, major milestones, and holidays are all up for deliberation. If you're feeling stuck for ideas, try closing your eyes and asking your loved one, "How would you like to be honored this year?" Sit in silence for a moment and see if any new revelations come to mind. Pin this list to your refrigerator or calendar, both to remind you of upcoming griefiversaries and to remember which rituals and traditions go with each date. Feel free to invite others to join in this list-making activity as they honor their own losses or celebrate your loved one with you.

"Because even through grief, we are growing." – SHELBY FORSYTHIA

When I first started doing grief work in 2016, I had the sense that something was happening, just below the surface, for me in my grief. I didn't have words for it at the time, but I know now that even in the dark tangle of years that was my life after the death of my mother, I was expanding, learning, and becoming more self-aware by the day. My life since the death of my mother has been anything but smooth and effortless, but I know that even in the midst of grief, there is growth, compassion, and love to be unearthed. Loss buries us underground, but our broken hearts hold the seeds for our inevitable regrowth. Your grief belongs to you. But so, too, does your coming back.

DECEMBER 31

DECORATE a clear, empty jar and place it next to your bed. Each night before you go to sleep, recollect one positive moment you experienced that day. This could be as small as "Noticed the birds in my backyard" or as big as "Survived [loved one's] birthday." Write your positive moment on a slip of paper, fold it up, and place it in the jar. Do this every day for a year. Then, this time next year, dump out and unfold your year's worth of positive moments. Not only will you experience an outpouring of warmth recalling positive memories from the previous year, you'll also form a more positive outlook toward the year ahead. Saturating your brain with evidence that positive things happened in the past gives it permission to dream up more positive experiences in the future. Sending comfort and love to you in the new year.

RESOURCES

The following websites and books can provide you with additional support in your life after loss. I know, because these are the resources that helped me in my own life. Of course, take what works for you and discard the rest.

WEBSITES

Work with a licensed therapist online via chat, phone, or video:

www.trybetterhelp.com/shelbyforsythia

Find grief support online or in person:

The Compassionate Friends
www.compassionatefriends.org

The Grief Recovery Method
www.griefrecoverymethod.com

Hospice Foundation of America
www.hospicefoundation.org

Make a will and learn to cope with the reality of your own death:

Going with Grace
www.goingwithgrace.com

Join guided workshops and communities
for reentering life after loss:

Refuge in Grief
www.refugeingrief.com

Second Firsts
www.secondfirsts.com

Read funny, poignant, and practical
stories on grief in the 21st century:

Modern Loss
www.modernloss.com

What's Your Grief?
www.whatsyourgrief.com

BOOKS

... IN NO PARTICULAR ORDER

Permission to Grieve, by Shelby Forsythia

A deep dive into undoing society's teaching about
grief and learning to honor our own.

On Living, by Kerry Egan

Reflective, inspiring accounts from a hospice chaplain's bedside.

Second Firsts, by Christina Rasmussen

One woman's journey to reenter life after the death of her husband.

Confessions of a Funeral Director, by Caleb Wilde

A touching selection of grief stories through the eyes
of a sixth-generation funeral director.

It's OK That You're Not OK, by Megan Devine

Validation and normalization of grief, especially the dark parts.

Modern Loss, by Rebecca Soffer and Gabrielle Birkner

Funny, poignant, and practical stories from grievers in the digital age.

Option B, by Sheryl Sandberg

Part memoir, part scientific study on life after a loved one dies.

When Breath Becomes Air, by Paul Kalanithi

A beautiful, tissue-worthy true story of a neurosurgeon's decline into death.

There Is No Good Card for This, by Emily McDowell and Dr. Kelsey Crowe

A witty illustrated guide for friends of grievers
on how to support a grieving person.

Grief Works, by Julia Samuel

A collection of relationship-specific (loss of a spouse, loss of a child, and so on) loss journeys seen through the eyes of a therapist.

Tuesdays with Morrie, by Mitch Albom

One man's account of his favorite teacher's end of life.

Advice for Dying Corpses (And Those Who Love Them), by Sallie Tisdale

Down-to-earth, human instruction on honoring a good death and creating one for yourself.

ACKNOWLEDGMENTS

A heaping armful of love to my community of wonderful Grief Growers, including my Patreon supporters, my clients and students, and my ever-expanding community of readers and podcast listeners. We are all walking one another home.

Big thanks to Dad, for firm foundations; to Susan, for bursts of cheer; to Paige, for parades of excitement; to Hattie, for invitations to play; to Lu, for rejoicing in the flow; and to Mom, for getting me here in more ways than one.

Endless gratitude to Tami, Emily, Gabby, and the Girl Gang, for never-ending hype and constant reminders to celebrate the wins.

Boundless appreciation to Meg, for reaching out; to Susan, for polishing the stone; and to Meredith, for tossing my hat into the ring.

Finally, a small, quiet thank-you to the griever I became on December 26, 2013. I exist today because you chose to live on. I am proud to carry you forward with me.

ABOUT THE AUTHOR

Shelby Forsythia is the author of *Permission to Grieve* and the podcast host of *Coming Back: Conversations on Life After Loss.* After the unexpected death of her mother in 2013, she became a "student of grief" and set out on a lifetime mission to explore the often misunderstood human experience of loss. Through her books, weekly podcasts, and one-on-one grief guidance, she helps grieving people find direction, get support, and cultivate radical self-compassion after devastating loss. Her work has been featured in the *Huffington Post, Bustle,* and *O, the Oprah Magazine.* Visit her website at shelbyforsythia.com.

Hi there,

We hope you found comfort reading *Your Grief, Your Way*.
If you have any questions or concerns about your book,
please contact **customerservice@penguinrandomhouse.com**
so we can take care of them. We're here and happy to help.

Also, please consider writing a review on your favorite
retailer's website to let others know what you thought
of the book and to help them with their buying decision.

Sincerely,
Zeitgeist Publishing